Bad Guys Don’t Have Birthdays

Bad Guys Don't Have Birthdays

Fantasy Play at Four

Vivian Gussin Paley

The University of Chicago Press

Chicago and London

The University of Chicago Press, Chicago 60637
The University of Chicago Press, Ltd., London

Paperback edition 1991
Printed in the United States of America

97 96 95 94 93 92 91 5 4 3 2

LIBRARY OF CONGRESS CATALOGING-IN-PUBLICATION DATA

Paley, Vivian Gussin, 1929–
Bad guys don't have birthdays: fantasy play at four/
Vivian Gussin Paley.
p. cm.
ISBN 0-226-64495-2 (cloth)
ISBN 0-226-64496-0 (paperback)
1. Child development. 2. Fantasy in Children. 3. Play.
I. Title.
LB1115.P19 1988
370.15′3—dc19 87-21748
CIP

∞ The paper used in this publication meets the minimum requirements of the American National Standard for Information Sciences—Permanence of Paper for Printed Library Materials, ANSI Z39.48-1984

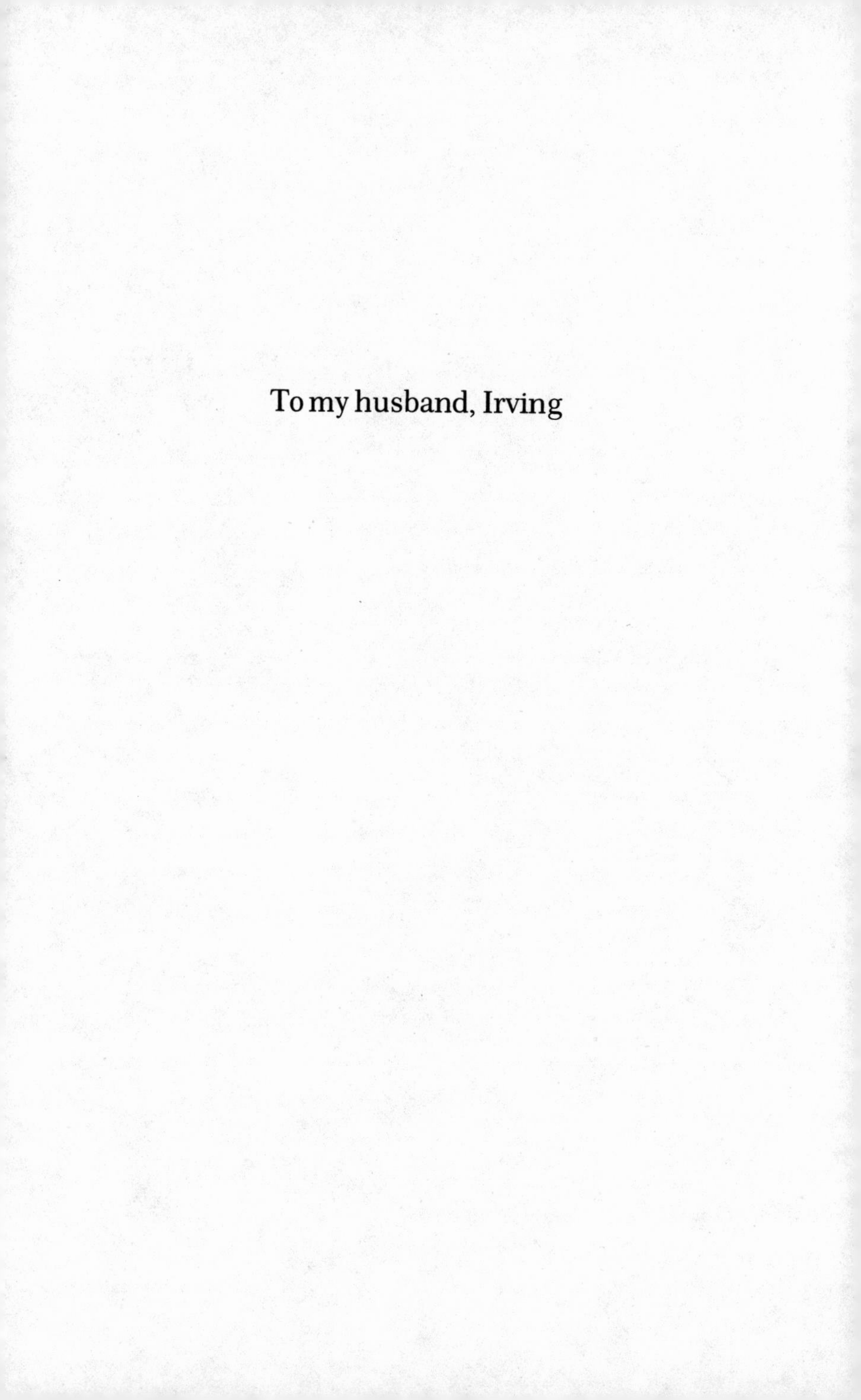

To my husband, Irving

Preface

I have come to this classroom of three- and four-year-olds to uncover their secrets, but the children seldom reveal them in conversation. Instead, they change identities and burrow into hidden places; they speak in code and flee from invisible foes; they manufacture problems whose resolution depends on judgments I cannot anticipate.

All year the fours have been announcing edicts for the containment of bad guys. Their rule-making is prodigious. Were I to impose prescripts at such a rate the children would withdraw in confusion, yet it is impossible for a child to suggest too many. The point seems to be to marshal a great fortress of laws, all of which may be contested, redrawn, and readministered with each new drama.

I record their fantasy play because it is the main repository for secret messages, the intuitive language with which the children express their imagery and logic, their pleasure and curiosity, their ominous feelings and fears. For the price of keeping order in the room I am privileged to attend the daily performance of private drama and universal theater that is called a preschool classroom.

This year three themes dominate the stage: bad guys, birthdays, and babies. What does it all mean? The magical rhythm that bounces back and forth between this odd triad is just beyond my reach; I can feel its presence but am hard put to identify the tune or carry the melody. One must be able to see through the disarray and concentrate on the drama.

Yet it is not simply a matter of concentration. When I *care* more about what the children say and think than about my own conventionality, those are the times I sense the beat and hear the unspoken lines. As I try to measure my responses to the forms and ideas of this emerging society that inhabits my classroom, it becomes necessary to grasp its point of view:

I pretend, therefore I am.
I pretend, therefore I know.

The reader may recognize Mollie and her friends whose initiation to school we followed in *Mollie Is Three*. Now they are four, and Fredrick's story becomes a central issue. The arrival of his new baby brother heightens the common perception of danger and loss, and we can examine the ways in which children use fantasy play to portray fear in order to prove that fear can be conquered: I pretend, therefore I am not afraid.

Joining Mollie and Fredrick center stage are Barney, Margaret, Emily, and Christopher, symbol makers and storytellers all. These six are the ones most studied and copied by their classmates. Mollie, who argued passionately at three that she was biggest, is now the stabilizing good mother, and Fredrick, last year's Incredible Hulk, will soon demand the infant's role with startling intensity. Barney is suddenly the competent leader, and, just as suddenly, Margaret appears uncertain and angry. Timid Emily invents villains and boyfriends, and anxious Christopher discovers the heady excitement of social competition.

How does the teacher who would study fantasy play find the main threads and weave an authentic pattern? By watching those who are watched. The group itself is the best judge of authenticity, choosing leaders who give voice to common concerns in the language and logic of their peers.

Each year, the talk, the play, and the stories reveal the same truths. Ideas and purposes must be processed through other children in social play if a child is to open up to an ever larger picture and determine how the pieces fit together.

The children in this book *play*; for them friendship and

fantasy already are broad avenues leading to questions and considerations that make sense to everyone. Listen to the process by which the children think about a subject and follow a theme along the intertwining paths of discussion, play, and storytelling. Fredrick, upon rehearing the tale of Jack and the Beanstalk, immediately makes an important connection for himself and the small group at the snack table. My role is somewhat akin to the ancient Greek chorus.

FREDRICK: Does the giant's wife like Jack?
TEACHER: She seems to. I wonder what Jack would say if she asked him to stay.
CHRISTOPHER: He said no. He said, "I gots a mother already."
TEACHER: But maybe the wife is lonely. What will she do?
PETEY: Buy a friendly fox.
JONATHAN: No, let her get a dog or a cat.
MOLLIE: They can live with Jack and his mother.
PETEY: And the cow.
BARNEY: They sold the cow and the mother would say no.
FREDRICK: She doesn't like bad guys.
TEACHER: Unless there is a way to change the giant to a good giant. I wonder if there is.
EMILY: A fairy godmother.
TEACHER: Like Cinderella's?
PETEY: She couldn't get in the door. Of that Jack and the Beanstalk place.

Moments later, the subject is examined in play:

FREDRICK: (*on the phone*) Jack, Jack, do you hear me?
BARNEY: Hello, do you hear me? You're too loud up there. I'm calling the bad guy place up there.
CHRISTOPHER: Someone knocked down the fairy. And also Jack's mother. Call the police. Hey, there's a robber. He might be big!

FREDRICK: Call the police. There's a whole bunch of things out there. It's danger. Tell Jack don't look up if there's a beanstalk. If his mother is sleeping.

There are more connections to be made, in yet another format. Fredrick dictates a story in which some central issues receive further attention: How safe is Jack? Can one fantasy enter another? Is Jack a superhero or just a little boy with a mother?

> Once there was Super Mighty Mouse. Once there was Superman. Superguy too. Then Jack came. Before Jack is going to climb up the beanstalk all the superguys chopped down the beanstalk. Then Jack looks inside all the superguys and all the pirates. And no one is there.

TEACHER: That's an interesting idea. Jack looked inside and no one was there.
FREDRICK: Because there was still standing the beanstalk. How could there be superguys? They're not even in Jack's story. Maybe he could visit.
TEACHER: Visit who?
FREDRICK: The giant's wife. If she's lonely.
BARNEY: He better not, Fredrick. I'm pretty sure that giant used to be her little boy.

Jack offers intriguing possibilities, but other topics go even further for these four-year-olds. Birthday, for example. Our story begins with Fredrick's analysis of his mother's birthday. The month is September, although it could be any other. Calendars seldom determine the fantasy play or the players. Bad guys, babies, and birthdays can happen at any time.

Bad Guys Don't Have Birthdays

1

"My mother doesn't have no more birthdays," Fredrick tells me in school one day.

"Do you mean she doesn't have a birthday party?"

"No. She really doesn't have a birthday. How I know is no one comes to her birthday and also she doesn't make the cake."

Fredrick is four and his ideas often take me by surprise. This is his second year in a classroom and my twenty-eighth.

"Do you think she still gets older every year?"

"You know how much she is old? Twenty-two."

His mother is older than that but Fredrick likes the sound of twenty-two. And Mollie's favorite is twelve-teen. "That's the olderest," she says. "My daddy is already a twelve-teener on his birthday."

I accept twelve-teeners and mothers who don't have birthdays as gifts. Each time a child invents one of these unique arrangements of image and phrase, I sense anew the natural order that gives young children this awesome talent for explaining life's mysteries. The thrill no longer comes from hearing my own answers repeated; I hunger for those I cannot imagine to problems unmentioned in the curriculum guides. Nearly every lesson I want to pursue arises out of the children's consciousness. Birthday is high on the list.

"Maybe you and daddy can make mother a birthday party," I suggest.

"But they never remember her birthday and when it's her birthday they forget when her birthday comes and when her birthday comes they forget how old she is because they never put any candles. So how can we say how she is old?"

"The candles tell how old someone is?"

"You can't be old if you don't have candles."

"Fredrick, ask your mother to have a cake and candles. She'll tell you when her birthday is."

"She can't because she doesn't have a mother. See, my grandma borned her once upon a time. Then she told her about her birthday. Then every time she had a birthday my grandma told her. But my grandma died."

I could tell Fredrick that of course his mother has a birthday, everyone has a birthday, but I know that to do so will merely put a halt to the conversation. He will not be convinced if he does not already believe it is true. Besides, he may have other reasons for depriving his mother of a birthday. She is about to have a baby and Fredrick has not yet acknowledged the fact. When Mollie asked him if his mother was growing a baby, he told her she was buying him a puppy.

Mollie eases in between us at the table. She knows when good conversations are in progress.

"Mollie, Fredrick says his mother doesn't have any more birthdays."

"Why not?"

"Because my grandma died and my mother doesn't know how many candles to be."

Mollie examines Fredrick's face. "Did your grandpa died too?"

"Yeah, but he came back alive again."

"Then your grandma told him. If he whispers it to your mother, maybe it's already her birthday."

"Why should he whisper, Mollie?" I ask.

"If it's a secret."

They understand each other. The necessary and universal aspect of birthday is not as appealing right now as their own theories, some of which Fredrick puts into stories for me to write down.

> Once came He-Man. Baby He-Man. The real He-Man told him it was his birthday. He didn't see Skeletor because it was a birthday.

"Because it was a birthday?" I ask.

"You don't see bad guys on your birthday."

"Hm-m. I wonder if bad guys see other bad guys on *their* birthdays."

"Bad guys don't have birthdays."

"Aren't they born on a certain day?"

"Bad guys don't have names so they can't have birthdays."

"You said his name is Skeletor."

"That's his pretend name."

Last year such information came from the older children in the class, but now Fredrick is in the "olderest" group and can invent some of the rules himself. My notebooks have begun to fill with the words of a new group of visionaries who have only recently discovered that they can surround their uncertainties and confusions with enough persuasive commentary to make the worry of the moment appear under control.

Christopher sits next to us, cutting "gold" out of yellow paper. We are at the story table, a large, round structure that is our central talking and listening and manufacturing place. You cannot pass from the blocks to the easels or from the doll corner to the sand table without noticing what is going on among the storytellers, picture makers, and paper shredders.

"Is that your pretend name?" Christopher asks.

"What name?"

"Fredrick. Is that pretend?"

"Yeah, it is."

"For hideouts?"

"Yeah."

Once again I am on the outside. "What do you and Christopher mean? Which name is pretend in a hideout? Isn't Skeletor the pretend name?"

"Not in a hideout."

I am learning to read their logic. When he is in character, Fredrick is the pretend name. Moments later, entering the doll corner, he assumes another disguise and continues some of his earlier inquiries.

"My baby just now jumped out, Fredrick," Mollie says. "Are you the daddy? It's already her tomorrow day's birthday."

"I'm the brother. Our daddy died because he sleeped too long in the day. Who is Barney going to be?"

"Barney could be the daddy. We need a dad," Mollie says.

"Okay, then the dad could come alive again. You want to, Barney?"

"I didn't come alive," Barney states firmly. "I was always alive. I just pretended I died because you didn't see me because I was at work."

Stuart runs in waving a cone-shaped plastic block. "Bang! Bang! Bad guys in the woods. Everyone get out of the woods!"

"No bad guys, Stuart," Mollie says. "There can't be bad guys when the baby is sleeping."

Whatever else is going on in this network of melodramas, the themes are vast and wondrous. Images of good and evil, birth and death, parent and child, move in and out of the real and the pretend. There is no small talk. The listener is submerged in philosophical position papers, a virtual recapitulation of life's enigmas.

Can any task be more important than monitoring these unexpected disclosures? Yet it took me half of my teaching career to take them seriously.

2

When I was twenty, I led a Great Books discussion group in the New Orleans Public Library. The participants were older and wiser, but my lists of questions made me brave.

Get the people talking, I was told, and connect their ideas to the books; there are no right or wrong answers.

The procedure seemed simple enough. I moved from question to question, and quite often it sounded as if it were a real discussion. Yet most of the time I was pretending. The people and the books were shadowy presences whose connections to one another seemed more real than their connections to me. What I wanted, desperately, was to avoid awkward silences.

Soon after, I became a kindergarten teacher and had curriculum guides instead of printed questions. I still believed it was my job to fill the time quickly with a minimum of distractions, and the appearance of a correct answer gave me the surest feeling that I was teaching. It did not occur to me that the distractions might be the sounds of the children thinking.

Then one year a high school science teacher asked to spend time with my kindergartners. His first grandchild was about to enter nursery school, and he wondered how he would teach such young students. He came once a week with his paper bags full of show and tell, and he and the children talked about a wide range of ordinary phenomena.

As I listened, distant memories stirred. "You have a remarkable way with children, Bill," I told him. "Their ideas keep coming and you use them all, no matter how far off the mark."

He laughed. "I guess it's not far off *their* mark. You know, the old Socratic idea? I used to be a Great Books leader up in Maine."

Watching him with the five-year-olds, I saw, finally, how the method worked. He'd ask a question or make a casual observation, then repeat each comment and hang on to it until a link could be established to a previous statement. He and the children were constructing paper chains of ideas, factual and magical, and Bill supplied the glue.

But something was going on more important than method: Bill was truly curious. He had few prior expectations of what kindergartners might think or say, and he listened with the anticipation we bring to the theater. He was not interested in what he knew to be an answer; he wanted to know how the children approached the problem.

"Incredible!" he'd whisper to me. "Their notions of cause and effect are incredible." And I, their teacher, who thought I knew the children so well, was often equally astonished.

I tried to copy Bill's open-ended questions, which followed the flow of ideas without demanding closure. But it was not easy. I felt myself always waiting for the right answer—my answer. The children knew I was waiting, and they watched my face for clues.

It was not enough to mimic another person's style. Real change, I was to discover, comes through the painful recognition of one's own vulnerability. A move to a new school in another city and an orientation speech by its director opened my eyes to an aspect of teaching I had not considered.

The director described a study done by two psychologists, Robert Rosenthal and Lenore Jacobson (*Pygmalion in the Classroom*, 1968), in which misleading information was given to several teachers about their students. In random fashion the children were labeled bright or not bright by means of fictitious IQ scores. The teachers, I was shocked to find out, asked more questions, waited longer for answers, and followed up more often with additional comments when they thought they were speaking to a smart child.

My shock was that of recognition: I could easily have been one of those unsuspecting teachers, though certainly I listened more to myself than to any of the children.

My problem went beyond the scope of the study, for even when I listened to the children I did not *use* their ideas. I paid attention only long enough to adapt their words to my plans. Suddenly, I wanted my role in the classroom exposed, but there were no Rosenthals or Jacobsons around eager to set up a privately incriminating study.

Then, miraculously, I discovered the tape recorder and knew I could become my own best witness. To begin with, it revealed why my discussions seldom had the ring of truth: I had not yet figured out *which* truths the children wanted to pursue.

3

Fredrick is at the playdough table when I refer again to his mother's birthday. In nursery school, no subject is ever finished.

"Maybe your mother doesn't have a birthday cake because she thinks cakes and candles are for children."

Fredrick shakes his head. "Uh-uh. She makes daddy a cake with candles."

"Can your father bake her a cake?"

"Fathers don't make cakes. They make popcorn."

"And blueberry pancakes on Sunday," Mollie adds.

Fredrick accepts Mollie's information with a nod and pauses to draw a large unsmiling face. Then he resumes the original topic.

"She thinked grandma will do it before she died." He stares at a spot on the table as he struggles with the shape of the coming sentences. "See, my grandma is her grandma's mother. My mother is the mother of the grandmother is the mother when she was little."

Whatever approach I use, Fredrick makes cause and effect of his grandmother's death and his mother's birthday. The matter is not unimportant, for the phenomenon of birthday looms large. It is one of the Great Ideas examined in play, along with cooking and eating, going to bed, watching for bad guys, caring for babies—the list is long.

But birthday is a central theme that cuts across the others, a study in number and identity, an investigation of friendship and power.

"You can't come to my birthday if you say that!"

"You *could* come to my birthday and my daddy will buy you a hundred pieces of gum."

Any observation concerning birthday is worth following, not in order to give Fredrick the facts and thereby close the subject, but to learn more about Fredrick and, perhaps, more about the meaning of birthday.

"Remember yesterday, Fredrick, when you were talking about your mother's birthday? You told Mollie your grandfather died and then he came alive again?"

"Yes."

"And then when Barney was the daddy he said he didn't come alive because he wasn't dead, he was only at work?"

"My grandpa is a doctor," Fredrick says, avoiding the issue. But it reemerges later when we read a book in which a boy pretends a friendly bear is his missing grandfather.

"Where is the grandfather?" Fredrick asks.

"The book doesn't tell us that," I answer.

"When he comes home the boy will be angry," he says.

"Because he wanted his grandfather to be at home waiting for him?" I ask. "Perhaps the grandfather was at work."

"I'll ask him."

Fredrick responds to questions about boys and grandfathers as if they are about himself and *his* grandfather. For more abstract views I must listen to Fredrick at play. Stepping into another role, he can imagine a variety of possibilities as he explains his pretend characters to other pretend characters. But I may need to guess at the premises.

What are the assumptions behind all the earnest explanations? When I taught in the kindergarten, the younger children so often responded to questions I did not ask, in a code I could not follow, that it became clear my perspective needed new lenses. I packed my tape recorder and moved to the nursery school.

Curiosity keeps me here, watching the three- and four-year-olds, for I still cannot predict the contents of their mysterious curriculum. But I am learning something about where the secrets are hidden; my new students disclose more of themselves as characters in a story than as participants in a discussion.

The tape recorder has lost its perch overlooking the kindergarten discussion circle and now trails along after the themes of itinerant nursery school players. My mechanical witness needs *me* to do the listening, but in the beginning, when I was learning to listen, the tape recorder was my instructor, the round-circle discussion my lesson book, and the kindergarten children my sometimes reluctant participants.

4

The problem was that I wanted to practice discussions and the children wanted to play. Their fidgeting and whispering too often became the subject of our discussions. I considered asking a colleague to sit in, but the prospect made me uneasy. Instead, I borrowed a tape recorder, and from the start the classroom took on a new life for me.

It was all there on the tape: the children's distraction and my displeasure, the voices struggling for attention, and the obscure murmurs hanging in midair. I confronted each day's tape with a mixture of dread and exhilaration.

Other facts began to appear. When anything was mentioned that had occurred during play, everyone snapped to attention. If an argument was recalled, or a scene of loss and despair was described, the class became unified in purposefulness. Annie complains that Kathy always has to be the mother, which reminds Sam that he doesn't like the mother pig because she made her children go into the woods where the wolf was. And, speaking of wolves, how come Paul every day tells Simon to be the bad guy or else he can't play? Is that fair?

These were urgent matters, and passion made the children eloquent. When the issues were fantasy, friendship, and fairness (I called them the three F's), the speakers reached to their outer limits to explain and persuade. No one wanted to leave the circle until justice prevailed.

However, the best was yet to come. In my eagerness to use the tape recorder I began to leave it on *after* the discussions and thereby made the most fruitful discovery of all. The subjects that inspired our best formal efforts were the same ones that occupied the free play, *and I was not needed as a discussion leader*.

The children were actors on a moving stage, carrying on philosophical debates while borrowing fragments of floating dialogue. Themes from fairy tales and television cartoons combined with social commentary and private fantasy to form a tangible script that was not random and erratic.

A relentless connection-making was going on, the children inventing and explaining their rules and traditions every time they talked and played. "Let's pretend" was a Socratic dialogue, and the need to make friends, assuage jealousy, and gain the sense of one's own destiny provided reasons for agreement on goals and procedures. An astonishing marketplace of ideas flourished in the kindergarten classroom, and I was just beginning to sample its wares.

In time I learned to conduct a lively discussion based on issues that seemed related to play. Yet I was bothered by the suspicion that I was still pretending, as in the old Great Books days. Was *my* subject really the children and *their* subjects? Did I not use their fantasies in order to have a good discussion, somewhat as I had once used Plato and

Aristotle because I needed something to talk about with a group of strangers in the public library?

In the midst of my incessant self-analysis, fantasy play itself has come to the rescue, for in nursery school it is a way of life that carries its own value and pursues its own course apart from any discussion of it. I am determined to follow the text of the play more closely this year in hopes of discovering why the children construct it as they do.

Besides, the younger children are not so easy to manipulate, and I can never be certain where the conversation ends and the fantasy play begins.

5

The curtain is up and the actors have entered the stage. This class, as all others have done, will produce scripts never before enacted, and the legends will evolve around those who attract the most curiosity about what they will say and do next.

"Hey, look! Teacher, look at me! I got on my daddy's Boy Scout shirt. Christopher, look what I'm wearing. You wanna build a Boy Scout ship? Huh, do you?"

The speaker is four-year-old Barney, and the shirt, a faded blue collage of circular symbols, hangs below his knees. Christopher twirls around between the tables, looking over his shoulders at the sway of his Batman cape, and seems not to hear Barney, who has already begun to build his ship.

"C'mon, Christopher. You can be Batman on my ship," Barney says. "Start building with me."

"*I'll* do it, Barn," Fredrick offers. "Let me be the guard."

Christopher is mobilized to attention. "No, Fredrick! No! He asked *me first*. Batman is the guard, didn't you say that, Barn?"

"Two people is okay for guards," Barney adjudicates.

"Then *you* hafta be a guard, Barn, not Fredrick."

"No, Christopher. That's *not* the way it hasta be. I'm the guy who controls the ship. I shoot the cannons because it was my idea first."

When Barney was three, he did not know "the way it hasta be." He and his friends often sounded like this when they played:

BARNEY: Emergency! Emergency!
MOLLIE: Fasten the seat belt! Down the bumper!

Tumbling out of an airplane made of blocks, they would run into the hallway and shout "Emergency!" down the stairs. A moment later the procedure was repeated, this time Mollie yelling "Emergency!" and Barney taking the "Fasten the seat belt" lines.

Fredrick and Emily invented a doctor routine that followed a similar rhythm.

FREDRICK: I broke my foot, mother. Call the doctor.
EMILY: (*dialing*) Hello, hello. Is this the doctor calling?
FREDRICK: (*rubbing his leg*) I'm fixing my own foot. Don't call the doctor.
EMILY: Are you still fixing your foot, father?
FREDRICK: I broke my foot again, mother. Call the doctor.

Remarkably, by the following September these emergency shouters and doctor dialers would step into complicated tales of pirates and princesses and sound as if they had always lived in a castle. Witnessing the phenomenon each year, I am no less in awe of this miracle of the imagination.

How do the brief dialogues of the three-year-old so suddenly merge, at four, into long, sequential dramas that connect multitudes of events into a single plot? From a two-person up-and-down rhythm come choruses of intriguers who circumvent, outwit, and disguise the unknown, the unwelcome, and the unacceptable.

The commissars of the past have moved on to kindergarten, and Barney and Mollie now wear the largest pieces of the mantle. They are followed closely by Fredrick, Christopher, and Margaret, who are fiercely jealous of their attentions. It is a painful dilemma and is part of the classroom drama. When the leading players act out the shape and fortune of jealousy, they are watched intensely, for no subject is more fascinatingly personal.

"Can't I be a Boy Scout?" Fredrick asks.

"Yeah, but I got a real one, don't forget."

"Me too," Fredrick counters. "This is a Boy Scout one I got on." He examines his striped pullover, which, for all he knows, may be a Boy Scout shirt.

"Just let's ask the teacher, Fredrick. Now look, teacher. *You* say who has the real Boy Scout shirt, me or Fredrick."

"The only kind I've ever seen is the one Barney is wearing."

Fredrick is momentarily checked. He can be a "guard" but apparently cannot call his shirt "Boy Scout." A year ago he might have cried or knocked down Barney's ship, but he has learned other ways to convince people he is right. "I mean I got one *under* this one. You can't see it because nobody can see it that's in school. Only if you're in my house. If you come to my house when it's my birthday you can see it."

"Am I coming?" asks Barney.

"Yes."

Barney hesitates. "Okay, we're both Boy Scouts. C'mon, we gotta build. The water is getting too high. There might be sharks."

The year before, everyone followed the bravura performances of Erik and John, unrelenting superheroes and inseparable friends. Our present heroes were then newcomers to school, and the exaggerated posturing of "the big boys" helped organize the long list of classroom demands around familiar issues. "The big boys" were good theater, to be wondered and worried and exalted over as one tried to make sense of school.

With the new cast of actors the text has changed. Barney and Mollie do not covet one exclusive friend or favor a single style of play; there is less dogma and more uncertainty and debate.

"How about me, Barney?" Christopher whines. "Why is he? No fair. I'm a real Boy Scout too."

"No you're not, Christopher. You know you're Batman. You even gots a cape. That's a very good thing to be. Batman could kill sharks. You got secret powers, okay? And I made you a bed."

"A bat bed? Make it a bat bed."

"Okay. You too, Mollie. Come over here, Mollie. I'm makin' you a bed the kind you like."

Mollie surveys the block scene. She likes to play with the boys and, as Barney knows, prefers beds to bombardments.

"Wait for me after I finish this what I'm doing," she calls. What she is doing is telling her daily Rainbow Brite story.

> Once Rainbow Brite came and then there was Lurky hiding and then Starlite came for her. Then Rainbow invited all her friends to her birthday. They had Rainbow Brite cups and Rainbow Brite plates and Rainbow Brite napkins and Rainbow Brite forks and Rainbow Brite spoons.

Each time she pronounces Rainbow Brite it is a caress, a magic intonation. Later, when we act out the day's collection of dictated stories, Mollie will dance around the room as I read out the list of party goods and very likely she will ask Christopher to be her faithful horse, Starlite, which is no small matter. These formal dramatizations of the children's stories take place before the entire class; powerful statements are made and repeated daily on the square of carpet we call a stage. Christopher is Mollie's friend, the class knows, because she always makes him

Starlite. And, whatever may happen on the Boy Scout ship, Christopher can rewrite the plot later in a story of his own, which, in fact, he does.

> The good Boy Scout that is Barney and me sees the alligator. Then they kill them with their swords. Then they go home together and sleep. Happily ever after.

For now, however, Christopher observes warily as Mollie drags a large blanket from the doll corner and drops it next to Barney, who inches over to give her more room.

Christopher lunges between them, dangling his black mask in front of Mollie's face. "Wait, Mollie, listen to me. I got everything for Batman. Everything!"

"So what, Christopher," Barney says. "Guess what, Mollie. I'm wearing my dad's Boy Scout shirt. And I got everything He-Man is supposed to have. Move, Christopher!"

"Yeah, move!" Fredrick joins in, quick to take advantage of an imbalance. "We're makin' money and you're not!"

"Whaddaya mean, you guys? I got real gold!"

"Those aren't money, Christopher. *This* is how you make it, right, Fredrick?"

Trembling in anger, Christopher holds up a fistful of paper. "I got more than you. I can get any piece of paper because you're not the boss!"

The boys glance furtively in my direction, wondering if the situation has deteriorated enough for me to interfere. The timing of my entrance is tricky, but tears usually work well with me. Today, however, Christopher keeps them from brimming over.

"What are you talkin' about? Mollie's never going to play with you. She's *my* friend. Mollie, Mollie . . ."

"Are you playing with him or us?" Barney demands.

"Say us, say us," Fredrick pleads.

Mollie purses her lips primly. "I'm still friends with the

whole of everyone. Nighttime, nighttime, everyone goes to bed. The rainbow is outside the window."

Miraculously, the tension dissolves. Rainbow Brite has accomplished what a teacher seldom can, the resolution of a conflict without disturbing the rhythm of the play. The children know when the emergency is over before I do; they reenter the fantasy so adeptly, it must be that the argument is part of the drama.

"Nighttime, go to bed," Barney coos. "Beddy-bye time."

"Wait, Barn." Christopher drops a crumpled wad of paper into Fredrick's lap. "Here's golden money for the morning. Put it in the bank."

"Not the bank, Christopher," Barney says pleasantly. "It's a Boy Scout ship. Did you forgot?"

"Oh, yeah, we're the guards. Are you still my friend, Barney?" Christopher is always the quickest to react to changes in the social barometer.

"Yeah, and you two are *guards*. *Guards,* don't forget. Make the gold in the morning so the jar will be full. When I wake up I might be He-Man."

Fredrick is surprised. "Can a Boy Scout be He-Man?"

"Are you kidding? A real Boy Scout can be anyone he thinks in his mind!"

Barney and his Boy Scout shirt have produced thirty minutes of highly focused, self-directed activity. I am hard pressed to imagine a project of my own that could so well occupy the hearts and minds of a group of four-year-olds.

And still the play continues; the climax of the Boy Scout story has not been reached. Act two, entitled "The Bad Guys," is about to begin.

6

No character is more rule-governed than the bad guy. In this class he cannot have a birthday or a name or share the stage with a baby. Once identified, he must be dealt with quickly. Are bad guys simply a convenient handle on which to hang rules and throw weight around? Or does their persistent intrusion signify a deeper purpose?

"Keep makin' gold," Barney orders. "You're the walkout guards and the goldmakers. Don't forget, I'm the guard that controls the guns."

"But we control the guns when you sleep," Fredrick decides.

"No. You make the gold and I control the guns. Anyway, I'm not sleeping because there's bad guys coming. Calling all guards! Stuart, get on. You wanna be a guard? Bad guys! They see the ship because it's already the sun."

"No bad guys, Barney," Mollie cautions. "The baby is sleeping."

"There hasta be bad guys, Mollie. We gots the cannons."

"You can't shoot when the baby is sleeping."

"Well, who *is* the baby? We didn't say a baby."

"It's Christopher," Mollie says. "Come on, baby Starlite. Lie down over here."

"Say no, Christopher," Barney urges. "You can be the Boy Scout brother. Say no, say no."

Christopher looks guiltily at Mollie. "I gotta shoot bad guys for a while, okay, Mollie?"

Mollie pulls the blanket around her shoulders. "Then I'm taking my blanket. Rainbow Brite is going to take care of some trouble things you don't even know it in a different place."

Predictably, the bad guy redefines the roles: the boys are more inclined to encourage his appearance and lengthen the stay; the girls would like him overruled or distracted en route. When there is an impasse, the girls usually adjourn.

"Why did Mollie leave the ship, Barney?" I ask in the ensuing pause.

"You can't have a baby if there's bad guys."

"Then why have bad guys?"

"They already saw the cannon. We have to shoot at them. Then we take them to jail. That's the whole real way. You can't say no bad guys if you already said bad guys."

Does Barney mean that once a bad or scary thought enters his mind, it is both necessary and logical to act it out? Mollie's sleeping baby was clearly a ploy; there had been no baby on the ship. A few days earlier, when Stuart entered the doll corner shouting, "Bad guy in the woods," Mollie was able to point out the impropriety of having a bad guy because a story involving a baby was already in progress.

The notion of an inherent logic in dramatic play would help explain the generally high degree of acquiescence when children first meet and begin to develop plots and assign roles. It is also the main reason I continue to make inquiries.

"How did you decide who could be a Boy Scout?" I ask as we walk upstairs to the music room.

"Someone that doesn't wear a cape," Fredrick says pointedly.

"I can take it off if I want," Christopher assures him.

"Do you want?" Mollie asks.

"No. In case of bad guys."

"Not in music, Christopher," I murmur hastily.

"He means he's thinking in his mind what if there's bad guys," Barney explains.

The boundary between "in his mind" and on the rug is thinly drawn, but the Great Books people would, I think, look with favor upon our discourse. Their injunction to discover the issues that keep people talking need only be rephrased to take into account that fact that play and not the printed book is the original source.

If play is the book, then the chapters turned to most often in this class deal with birthdays, bad guys, and babies. These three leitmotifs are pivotal to the daily drama and perhaps to intimations of reality itself. Because of them the child must find out who controls the fantasy, the players or their disguises. Children who are able to state that bad guys don't wake up babies or come to birthdays are ready to impose rules on the random tyranny of their fantasies.

There are persistent connections between the bad guy, the baby, and the birthday that have begun to occupy my attention. Certainly all three are tied to changes in the emotional climate. The bad guy, in particular, is a weather vane of mood and feeling, and the children seem to use him (once they are no longer used *by* him) to diffuse their personal demons.

In the theater, the bad guy plays the same role, but these children have not been taught by a printed script. Their sources are deeper; they may be the wellspring of all imaginative thinking.

7

There are moments of truth in the classroom that illuminate a particular aspect of the child's inner world and forever change my perspective. Such a revelation occurs during a story told by Emily, and the subject is bad guys.

The unexpectedness of the source only magnifies the impression, for few children would be less likely to talk about bad guys. Emily plays mothers and sisters going shopping, and she tells stories about little girls and friendly hippos.

This day, however, she announces that she is Teela, superfriend of He-Man.

> A little girl went over the hill. Then Teela came.

Emily smiles as she plans the next sentence. Filling the silence, I say, "Ah, Teela. She's never been in your story before. Which reminds me: Your sister always put Cinderella in her stories."

It is a gratuitous comment, to be sure, but Emily's response astonishes me. Her voice is suddenly loud and raspy. "Oh, mine's not that one. But I can tell you that one about Cinderella."

> Once Cinderella came. And then Cinderella died. Cinderella is killed. And then Teela fighted the bad guys and she kicked them and she killed them also. And then she punches them also. And she goes to sleep and when she wakes up it's her birthday.

Emily turns to leave the story table, but I draw her back.

"What happens to Cinderella?"

"Nothing."

"Doesn't Teela save her?"

"No. She's just killed."

"She doesn't come alive later?"

"No, no. Not that either."

A casual reference to her sister at the moment when mild-mannered Emily is about to divulge her own superhero fantasy brings forth bad guys with such alacrity I must assume they have never been far away. This bad guy character is more than just masculine bombast if Emily uses him so naturally to eliminate her sister.

When we act out Emily's story, I watch Mollie closely, remembering how upset she was the year before when Barney told a story in which Mr. McGregor eats Peter Rabbit. This led to a whole genre of male storytelling that toppled traditional endings: the troll captured the littlest billy goat and Jack became dinner for the giant. Mollie and Emily complained loudly as each new version was put on stage, and for a time the boys' heresies and the girls' accusations were part of the classroom ethos.

Cinderella is a greater favorite, yet Emily's woeful tale does not displease Mollie. It is three-year-old Dana who protests.

"Cinderella has glass slippers, Emily," she says. "You didn't do the dancing part."

"This is a bad Cinderella," Emily explains to Dana. "They *don't dance*."

Last year, all the male heroes had bad-guy counterparts: bad He-Man, bad Superman, bad Luke. In this class baby He-Man is a more likely alternative, yet Emily invents a bad Cinderella with the confidence of one who knows all the secrets of good and bad.

Within the hour I have another opportunity to speculate about bad guys as Christopher sets the scene for himself and Mollie in the doll corner. With the same speed Emily musters in disposing of Cinderella, Christopher identifies and demolishes *his* unwanted character.

"Listen to this, Mollie," he begins. "I'm sleeping down with Rainbow Brite. I can sleep with you when we go to sleep again tomorrow. Not the real day tomorrow."

"But *I'm* Rainbow, did you forgot?"

"Oh, then *this* is the pretend tomorrow. Look at the beautiful sun."

"I'll cover you over your little furry part," Mollie says, tucking in the blanket across his hair.

Fredrick stands at the head of the bed and lifts a corner of the blanket. "Is Christopher sleeping? Can I play?"

"No, I'm dead. That's the problem."

"Give him this magic drink, Mollie. He'll come alive." He hands Mollie a wooden cylinder.

"This is poison mud, doggy," she says, patting Fredrick's head. "You're my doggy that finds the poison mud."

Christopher jerks up his head. "No, Mollie. We don't even have a doggy. Fredrick can't play. That doggy we used to have got dead from a tiger."

"Oh, yeah?" Fredrick sneers. "Well, guess what? *I'm* that tiger. Gr-r-r! You're the one that got eated, Christopher!"

Christopher begins to cry. "Call the teacher, Mollie. Teacher, teacher, hurry! He's spoiling it what we're doing!"

"What are you doing that he's spoiling?" I ask.

"I'm dead from poison mud but I'm asleep and there isn't no tiger but he just thinked there is."

"I'm Battle Cat," Fredrick says.

"We're not playing He-Man," Mollie states.

"Meow, meow. Baby Battle Cat. That's a kitty, you know, Mollie." Fredrick purrs and licks his paw.

"And I'm still dead," Christopher says, covering himself up again. "I have to be dead a long time and when I wake up I'm the new baby Starlite."

Reviewing the plot: Christopher, made unhappy by Mollie's attentions to Fredrick, tries to eliminate him by invoking a tiger. Whereupon, Fredrick becomes the tiger and frightens Christopher. The themes are jealousy and rejection, and the tiger has a legitimate role. He enables the boys to vent their anger and then brings in the teacher to help close the act.

Would the peace have been undisturbed had Fredrick not happened by? Perhaps so, but the following morning, when Mollie and Christopher resume their play, a different crisis is precipitated and the issues are very nearly the same.

"No poison mud today, Starlite. Go to sleep."

"I finished sleeping. Now I have to go to work, mother."

Mollie grabs his arm. "Don't go. Stay in bed with the baby. I'll wake you up when the alarm clocks."

"I got my tie on already. I saw the day. I'll be right back, Mollie. I just gotta go over there in Barney's car for one short time. I got to ask can I be the driver."

Mollie is upset. "Stay here, father. I hear a noise in the chimney."

"Then it's the wolf," Christopher says. "I'll get the bullets."

"No, get under here with me."

"Bang! Bang! Bang! Hey, you're the wolf, Fredrick," Christopher shouts. "You're dead. I just shotted you."

"Yeah? I came alive. Gr-r-r. No one can kill me." He crawls about knocking over chairs, clawing at the dishes and playdough.

Nothing brings me quicker than dumping, except perhaps crying. No one is crying, but the decible level is high. "Fredrick, really! Look at this mess. What are you playing?"

"They said I'm the wolf."

"He's a different wolf that got eated up," Mollie explains. She has already begun to reset the table.

"Am I still the father, Mollie?" Christopher asks. "Are you my friend?"

"I'm the both of your friend," she says, pressing out heart-shaped cookies. "You can both come to my birthday."

Mollie purports to dislike any tumult that might wake the baby, yet deliberately manufactures her own scare the moment she worries about Christopher going off to play with Barney. Mollie, the sought-after one, the confident one, succumbs as easily as the others to the fear of abandonment.

If a fear cannot be avoided, the children seem to be saying, then make it the central issue, let it surface and explode. Act out the ominous feelings so the play can continue. And continue it does, as if there had never been a wolf in the chimney.

"I'm home, mother. Ding-dong."

"Bring the baby's medicine, father."

"Am I the baby?" Fredrick asks.

"The brown doll is the baby. You're the cooker."

Fredrick begins to stir the pot, then remembers

something he wanted to tell Mollie. "Guess what! This is real. It's Prince Adam's birthday. On television!"

"How 'bout pretend *you're* Prince Adam?" Mollie suggests. "I'm She-Ra but she's also the mother and Christopher can be our child."

"No, pretend I'm baby He-Man," Fredrick says, "but I didn't come alive yet so you don't see me."

"Whoosh!" Christopher waves a spoon. "Whoosh! Now you're alive. I made you be alive. Hi, there, you just now got borned."

Fredrick frowns, remembering another fact of his life. "Wait! That borning didn't happen. There are *no new babies* anymore! I'm only the same baby He-Man that was here already!"

Some wolves slide down chimneys and others appear in receiving blankets. Fredrick's mother came to school today looking as if the baby might arrive at any moment. But the event remains a secret in the classroom, unless one cares to read between the lines spoken by baby He-Man.

I like to read between the lines. Sometimes I listen into and around the same line several times: the original, its replay on the tape, and such follow-up dialogue as may occur.

"I noticed before that you were baby He-Man," I say to Fredrick.

"I was."

"You said there are no new babies anymore."

"Yeah, because baby He-Man is still going to be a baby."

"Maybe when he grows bigger there will be a baby. Do you think so, Fredrick?"

"If he's not bigger there won't be."

"How big, I wonder."

"He has to have his birthday."

My intention, when I began this pattern of repeating what the children say, may have been to secure a more accurate tape, but I soon realized how much the children wanted to hear their own and their classmates' lines again. All the children could better explain and expand an idea upon a second hearing. In effect, I was their playback, and they studied our dialogues-in-the-making as I would later review them on tape.

"What're you talking about?" Christopher wants to know.

"I was remembering what Fredrick said before when he was baby He-Man and you were the father."

"What did he say?"

"That there were no new babies. Only baby He-Man."

Christopher remembers the conversation. "But there hafta have some babies, Fredrick," he says. "In a different family. Not baby He-Man."

Fredrick nods. "I know. Or you can't be older. Hey, y'wanna play that again?"

They race off to the doll corner. I would like to hear more about "you can't be older," but for now my part is over.

8

Fredrick's note says his grandmother will pick him up today. She has come to stay, it explains, while his mother is in the hospital.

I read the note to him and then to Mollie, who asks to hear it. "Is that your grandmother the one that died?" she wonders.

"That one still died. This is Grandma Sarah. She's coming so she can take me to the zoo."

Neither child mentions the part about the hospital. "Ask her if I can come too," Mollie says. " 'Cause I never been there before. Only two times."

"First I gotta do a story for her. My daddy said to tell a nice story to show my grandma."

Fredrick needs no encouragement to tell stories these days; he has been dictating two every day, each one "badder" than the one before. "Hey, Emily, you want to hear my story? This is diffinter from last time. Much badder."

"Like mine? Teela?"

"A hundred badder," he replies. Emily moves closer, her chin resting on his shoulder. She wants more information about bad things.

> Once there was a knight that was the king's friend. And there was another knight. And there was a friend who was sometimes bad called Rhinoceros. And then they fighted and they bleeded.

"When is he bad?" Emily asks.

"If he's a good guy he fights the bad guys and when he's a bad guy he doesn't fight. He just stays."

"Bad guys don't fight?" I ask, surprised.

"You're wrong, Fredrick," Barney calls from the sand table. "Bad guys *do* fight."

"I mean they do fight but then they don't fight." Fredrick is trying to make a statement about bad guys but cannot find the right words. "Well, I gotta do my story some more."

> And then there was a huge enormous dragon and the dragon was the knight's friend. A king's knight's friend. And there was a kind of giant that was the knight's friend. And they have a feast on Skeletor. He died until he was dead.

Fredrick circles the table twice and is back at my side again. "Bad guys *do* fight," he says.

"So you agree with Barney, then."

"I mean he won't really fight. He'll go on the other team and fight the other bad guys and if he's a good guy he'll just go on the other team, the *other* ones, not the first ones."

"I think you mean bad guys fight each other," I suggest.

Emily has a different answer for Fredrick. "I know why they don't like each other. Not the part about teams. Because the good guy has something the bad guy wants it and he tries to *steal* it."

"Oh, the gold!" Fredrick remembers with renewed confidence. "Oh yeah, see, if you're good you always got the things they want. That's why they stop fighting because he's busy stealing your gold."

"Not from good guys, Fredrick," Barney says.

"Why not?"

"Because good guys have special things they could hide things."

"Like pirates?" Fredrick asks. "Y'wanna be that, Barn? Pirates?" He jumps up, eager to stop a confusing discussion and, instead, examine the contradictory visions in action. "Good pirates, I mean. C'mon, we need lotsa stuff and things. From the doll corner."

That which Fredrick has been unable to explain in conversation unfolds comfortably in play. This is the plot: pirates rob the doll corner but cannot themselves be robbed because they are good guys. To make doubly certain there are no violations Barney becomes a baby seal. "If I'm a baby," he says, "there won't be any bad guys."

No matter how often I hear these injunctions I am impressed by the intuitive logic of play. At some point between three and four the children learn that, even though powers do exist beyond their ken, they can nonetheless order a universe that makes sense and is under their control. This is what the good-bad pirates are about to do.

"Don't make a noise. Steal all this stuff in here," Barney whispers. His tip-toe entrance seems unnecessary since the doll corner is empty.

"We need more dishes, Barn, in case those get dirty." Fredrick fills a big straw purse with plastic plates, stopping only to cover his head and most of his face with a grey fedora. "And we need guns. Pirates has to have three guns: one in my hand, one in my shirt, one in my shoe."

"Look, Fredrick," Christopher breathes heavily. "Rich gold and lots of real money. Pretend this is the hideout. I'm the boss because it was my idea."

"Robbers!" Fredrick shouts. "Hide the drinks."

"You don't have to," Barney reminds him. "Good guys *don't* hide drinks. Nobody can't steal from good guys."

"But, Barn, what if strangers come in the nighttime?"

"They *know* not to steal these."

Christopher is not convinced. "They might not even know we're good guys. Cover it with this board."

"Never mind. I'm a baby seal now," Barney says, coughing out seal noises. "B-k-k! B-k-k-k!"

"I'll be the daddy seal," Fredrick is first to say.

"I'm the dad first," Christopher claims a moment later.

"Two dads, you guys. B-k-k! B-k-k-k!"

"Here's your best dad, baby seal. You like me best, right, Barn?" Christopher moves in front of Barney, blocking his view, but Fredrick pushes him aside.

"Stop sayin' you're the best, Christopher! I'm the He-Man dad. I got powers! You want me to build you a gun, baby seal? I'm the only dad that can do that for you."

"Babies don't have guns," Barney says.

"Then how will you fight the bad guys?"

"Now look, if I'm the baby there won't be any bad guys. I *told* you. Stop makin' up the wrong ideas."

At this point, Mollie and Margaret return to the doll corner. They have been out "shopping," each in a wide-brimmed hat and frilly bed jacket. "Sh! Don't lie down there, Barney. My babies have to be put to bed right now."

"Mollie, let me be your baby," Barney chirps in a tiny voice.

"No, Barney. Get out! The dolls are the babies. If you use dolls there can't be persons. No, Barney! Don't lie there!"

Barney is visibly offended. "Hey, Fredrick, get in the oven and I'll burn you up." He opens the oven door and laughs raucously, dumping Mollie's cookies on the floor.

"They can't play with us, right, Margaret?"

"Yeah, we'll rob you," Barney shouts. "Calling all bad guys and robbers. Steal this lady's children!"

"Teacher, teacher, we were here first!"

The pattern is remarkably consistent. As soon as a character feels displaced, he creates a distraction which then must be tested and counteracted. Christopher claims to be the boss of the hideout, and so Fredrick hears robbers, who lose credibility the moment a baby seal surfaces. A dispute over paternal loyalty brings on He-Man, but he also must step aside for the baby. Finally, when Mollie rejects Barney, the seal family become robbers. Nearly every alteration in the plot expresses discontent or renewal—and gives me a subject for discussion.

"I'm curious about something you said before, Barney. That good guys don't have to hide things because no one can steal from them."

"Bad guys have to steal from other bad guys."

"Well, I'm not sure Fredrick agrees with you. He thought strangers might come and steal the drinks."

"They can't," Barney says. "Because they're pretend and we're real."

"Real seals?"

"Real that you can see."

"But what if Stuart pretends he's the stranger? Then we can see him too."

"No. Because we had the blocks first. He has to ask."

When the logic of his fantasy fails, Barney invokes school rules. But he would rather give the power to a baby seal and maintain control over the fantasy. For all their rules and regulations the children worry that the creatures they invent may have lives of their own.

This is made clear during an impromptu story of mine, intended to fill a few spare moments at the end of the day. Rosabel, my heroine, has just received new birthday clothes from her grandparents and is returning home through the woods. She is accosted by Bear, Wolf, Fox, and Rabbit, each in turn demanding a present. The moment

Rosabel gives her purple bonnet to Bear, Emily jumps up and cries, "Don't let anyone take the red velvet gown!"

"All right, Emily, not the gown," I promise, but she reminds me with every new sentence. "Don't let anyone take the red velvet."

"Emily, listen. *I'm* making up this story. If I say no one will take the gown then it can't happen. But here's what *will* happen: Grandfather will come soon and tell all the animals to give back the presents."

"Do it now," Emily whispers.

She is not alone in her doubts; others look concerned. Who has more power, the storyteller or the story? I decide to conclude quickly: "Then Grandfather scolded the animals and told them to give back all the presents. Rosabel put on her pretty clothes, and when she and Grandfather got home her mother was waiting with a birthday cake and candles."

"I don't like that story," Emily says when I finish.

"I know. But I didn't think it would be so scary."

"It wasn't. Just Rosabel was scared."

9

I should have provided more protection for Rosabel: polite, flower-picking animals who say "Please," or a mother with a pail of blueberries. A conscientious mother, in fact, can disband any number of bad guys, as Mollie proves the next day in a doll corner hideout. With one sharp maternal admonition she causes a complete turnabout in the action.

"He-Man!" Barney shouts, holding up a frying pan. "Hey, why don't we move the furniture to be a hideout?"

"I smell a human," Christopher sniffs. "Let's get in the hideout."

"We gotta move this stove. Help me, Christopher. It's a

hundred heavy." Barney grunts and pushes. "I smell Skeletor coming to destroy the world. Get the chair up here, Fredrick."

"Someone's coming," Fredrick mutters gruffly. "Somebody's stealin' houses, huh, huh. Hey, pretend *we're* the bad guys and *we're* stealin' the house."

Mollie enters, puts on the silver slippers and rose-flowered hat, then turns to glare at the boys. "Oh no! I don't *believe* it. A chair could break, Barney, do you realize that? Do you? And guess who has to pay for it? If you break it. *You* do, you will have to pay for the *whole* chair."

"Because it's a light thing for it?" Barney asks.

"Yes! And you're the one. And also," Mollie says, looking at each boy, "there is too much noise in here. Simply *too* much. That's why I came home early."

Instantly, the three boys change from robbers to babies. "Wa-ah, wa-ah, mommy, mommy."

"I asked you to be quiet but you won't because you're just making noise. If you be quiet! Go to sleep."

"Where can I sleep, mommy?" Barney whines, surveying the jumble of furniture in the center of the room.

"Sleep in the white bed because it has no pillow because somebody took the pillow. And don't anybody sleep on a bump if they have a bump or you'll break your bones and then you'll be sorry. Now I say go to sleep. Turn off the lights this minute!"

"Yes, mommy."

"And everybody can't play either with the lights. You're wasting electricity and guess who has to pay for it. *You*. Don't you know you have to buy a light bulb?"

He-Man, Battle Cat, and Skeletor have disappeared under the weight of maternal directives. As Mollie strides about the doll corner adding blankets to her bedded-down family and dress up clothes to herself, she surrounds the players with the comforting banter of adult concerns: Don't waste electricity, sleep on a bump, or break chairs. Swinging a large purse on her arm, she issues a final warning. "And *don't* step on a crack. They might have thumb tacks and they could stick in your feet. And don't blame me."

A few days later, Mollie plays another scene in which bad guys are subdued by altogether different means. Confronted by Barney, Christopher, and Stuart as she begins to build a Rainbow Brite house, she beguiles the boys with tender invitations.

"Hey, Mollie, you took too much blocks. We need to make a hideout."

"Everyone come in here, won't you please? We're ready to travel. I packed this picnic for our pizza picnic. This house is almost finished for you, you, and you!"

"Watch out for us, Mollie," Barney says. "We're bad guys."

Mollie rearranges some blocks. "There. Everyone can sit where they want. But don't push down the pizza. It's very delicate and very tasty in the mouth."

"It's poison," Barney growls.

"Yeah, for the bad guys." Christopher mimics his tone.

"Sit, sit, sit, sit, have a pizza-rizza-pizza-pie," Mollie sings. "Pizza pie oh my."

"Mollie, I'm Trap Jaw," Barney informs her seriously. "He's a bad guy, you know."

"Oh hi, Trap Jaw. You need some food?"

"I'm a *bad* guy."

"Take some food, Trap Jaw. It's Trap Jaw food to have a picnic." Mollie has been wrapping small blocks in paper. "First come the lettuce samiches."

"I mean we're really good guys," Barney says, and Christopher neighs. "Ne-eh-eh. I'm Starlite, Mollie. Look at me. I'm your little horsie."

Do bad guys admit to being good just so they can attend a picnic? "I didn't think bad guys went to picnics," I comment later to Barney.

"This is my cowboy hat," he tells me, pointing to the large hat he has worn all morning.

"Then you weren't really Trap Jaw?"

"That was something I dress up when bad guys are there. It's a Trap Jaw hat and also a cowboy hat."

Mollie touches the felt band on the hat. "If Barney wears this they'll think he's Trap Jaw," she says encouragingly. "Because they don't know it's very soft." Another rule: *soft* is for good guys.

"*Pretend* Trap Jaw, Mollie. Real Trap Jaw doesn't go on picnics, you know."

How does Mollie know when Trap Jaw is *pretend* and can be invited to picnics? Or does the picnic itself confer the elevated status? If appearance is everything, then doing what good guys do makes you a good guy. I test the idea at my next opportunity, but it does not work; I have misjudged cause for effect.

The sounds of real anger have brought me into the doll corner, where Christopher has confiscated all the blankets and is screaming at Fredrick.

"Don't come on here, Fredrick!"

"I need this! You can't push me off."

"It has to be for *everyone*," Barney orders, "and don't push someone."

"Boys, boys, stop fighting right now. What's happened? Why does everyone look so angry?"

Christopher dissolves into tears. "I said I was Trap Jaw and then Barney said Care Bear because he wants Fredrick to be Trap Jaw and I need all these blankets because I had them first and I'm under a mountain by myself." His last words are swallowed in a new torrent of crying.

"We weren't playing He-Man anymore," Barney mumbles. "It's a birthday."

"Can't Trap Jaw come?" I ask.

"Not to a birthday."

"See, I told you," Christopher sobs.

"But Barney, why can't Christopher be the *pretend* Trap Jaw the way you were at Mollie's picnic?"

"No bad guys."

"If you invite him to the birthday he won't be a bad guy. Isn't that how you play?"

"Not every time we don't." He looks away guiltily.

"I'm not playing with Barney ever!" Christopher runs into the cubby room and I follow him. "And he's not coming to my birthday," he adds, burying himself under a pile of sweaters and jackets.

"Don't cry, Christopher. Come on, let's play dominoes, okay? The new ones you like?"

He uncovers his tear-streaked face. "And don't let Barney play with those. He's not my friend."

By snack time they are friends again, and I am somewhat wiser. Had the boys wanted Christopher to play they would have called him baby Trap Jaw or pretend Trap Jaw. Picnics and birthdays do not in themselves initiate the era of good feeling; they announce that the rhythm has already reached an upswing. The bad guy disappears when he no longer serves a purpose.

10

If I cannot easily change bad guys to good guys, the reverse is unfortunately a simple matter to accomplish. When my need for order prevails over the logic of fantasy, I can be as disruptive as Skeletor.

Barney and Fredrick have been hauling hollow blocks past me at an increasingly rapid rate, crying, "Fish for sale!" when I realize suddenly that the "fish" are being dumped on the doll corner floor.

"I want blue fish," Mollie says agreeably.

"Okay. I'm going to unloose you a blue fish." Barney struggles with the polka dot tie that is his fishing line and drops a block at Mollie's feet with a loud thud.

"Don't bring any more blocks in there, boys," I call out from the story table. "It's already a mess. And please don't drop them like that. The blocks are getting chipped." I sound a bit like Mollie warning the boys about the cost of electricity.

"These isn't blocks," Fredrick tells me. "It's fish. We're fishermen."

"People need those to build with," is my curt response. "Use something else, can't you?"

"These are gooder. You could tie them up and catch as much as you can."

"But look at the doorway, Fredrick. Nobody can walk into the doll corner."

"Mollie can walk, can't you, Mollie? She *likes* this kind of fish with a big open mouth, see?" Fredrick appeals to reason, but I have pulled back, unreachable.

"Blocks are simply too big to cook. Let Mollie use the plastic shapes. They'll fit nicely into the frying pan."

Barney listens to the debate with a deepening frown. "These are *sharks*. They hasta be boiled in the chimney," he says defensively.

Chimneys and sharks should alert me to a mood change but I am too bothered to hear the message. "Just put them back, would you please? It's not a good way to use the big blocks."

Why not admit that the blocks do look like big open-mouthed fish? I am determined, it seems, to make ordinary play into negative behavior. Alternatives crowd my mind: give them a fish basket, suggest a fish market, make them some paper fish. Better yet, wait patiently for the inevitable turn in the plot: the doll corner players are bound to become annoyed at the unwieldy pile of blocks, and, in response, the fishermen will steal back the fish. Or perhaps, the blocks will be used to build a chimney in the doll corner.

My solution is an unimaginative cleanup job, ending the play. Well, not quite. Despite my efforts, group spirits are about to be revived.

"Hey, Barn, ya wanna make a war boat?" Fredrick asks, unloading the last of the blocks.

"Yeah, a *bad* war boat. We gotta kill all the whole sharks there is."

"Look what I got here," Fredrick whispers, peering sideways at me. "I got the story paper. It's a bunch of gold. Don't show her."

"We're stealin' stuff, right? Bang! Bang!"

I note with dismay that my impatience has affected nearly everyone in the vicinity. The boys are in a war boat with purloined story paper, and the doll corner has emptied of all its original players, who are now seated at the painting table. Mollie dashes off a tricolor rainbow, then approaches the war boat.

"Can I play? I'll be a good person."

Fredrick shakes his head. "You gotta be a fighting person who fights with the war."

"I think this might be a house," Mollie says invitingly.

"It's not," Barney insists. "We have to have a war. Inside the water. Not on land."

"But look what I brang, Barney." Mollie empties the contents of a small box. "I'll be a good war person who has three tiny chicks and three tiny egg houses. Guess which chicken?" She arranges three plastic shells on the war boat and puts a fuzzy chick under each shell.

"I guess this one!" Barney lifts the shell eagerly.

"Right you are!" Mollie screams. "Did you get surprised?"

Stuart is even more excited. "Let me guess, Mollie. This one. I got it!"

"Right you are, Stu. Fredrick, you could guess that one. Go ahead, pick it up. Right you are, bumble bee. You all winned the game."

No one's pleasure is diminished by the fact that each chick has been placed under its shell in full view. "Guess" is taken to mean "look." The name of the game is *certainty*, not *chance*.

"Now *you* have to guess, Mollie." Barney replaces each chick under its same color shell.

"This one, this one, this one," Mollie squeals. "Feel them, they're so soft. They're looking for food. Peck, peck,

peck. Pretend this is the chicken house, Barney. I'm the mommy chicken, okay?"

"It's a war boat, Mollie."

"But just *pretend* this is the chicken good war boat." She hops the chicks in and out of their shells. "This is the chicken house over here, where we eat."

"Mollie, listen," Barney says. "Pretend that place is the other part and the chickens could come over here if they want but not when it's a war, okay? Pretend we have to ride to the war. Here we come."

"Me and my chickies will help you, Barney. You're going to the food store. You get the food, Barney. And here's all the food you need. I'm bringing you some presents, too, Christopher, from Milwaukee. That's why I was so late because I was walking so fast. It was a long, long way to the picnic."

Mollie's monologue gives a gentle rhythm to the block building. Good and bad guys move back and forth between war boats and chicken houses, guns and picnic supplies. It is a magical thing, this rhythm, and worth pursuing. I cannot manufacture it, but when I enter its sphere it is not unlike stepping into a deep forest and listening to the birds sing.

11

Mollie dictates a chicken story.

> Once came three chickens. Then they had a egg to live in that was their house. Then they ate breakfast. Then they went to the park to play. Then a little cat came and said, "I'll be nice to you and I won't eat yourself. I'll be your mom since you don't have a mom."

Throughout her story, Mollie plays with the chicks, covering and uncovering them, smiling each time a chick appears. "Do you like to play this game, teacher?"

"How do you play?"

"It's not too hard for you. You have to guess which chicken."

"Do I guess which *color* chicken is under the shell?"

"Guess which *chicken*."

"Guess if there *is* a chicken in there?"

"No. Which chicken. *What* chicken."

"All right. I guess this one."

"Right you are! You guessed a good job, teacher."

"Mollie, can I show you a different way to play? Watch. I put a chick under *one* shell but not under the others. Then I keep moving the shells around so they're all mixed up. Then you try to guess where the chick is. Okay? Try it."

Mollie looks doubtful. "They're very delicate. When you move them."

"I'm doing it gently, Mollie. Don't worry. Move, move, move, move. There. Now, guess which one."

She lifts the shell nearest to her hand and is startled to find it empty. "Where is it? Where's my chicken?"

"Under a different shell. Try another."

She shakes her head. "That's not the really way. My chicks want to be in their house if you want to guess."

"You like your game better."

"Mine is the really game because the chickens have houses to be in their houses."

Our games have little in common. My game represents loss and displacement, the chicks bereft of home and comfort. Mine is the wolf at the door, the shark nipping at the boat. Mollie's "really game" is the mother on the hearth and the baby in the crib.

Our views are far apart in games, and tomorrow, in real life, the gap will be even wider. That is the day I stamp my foot and fly into a tree.

12

The moment his mother opens the car door, Fredrick explodes with information. "A terrible really bad thing happened, not pretend, and the teacher was so mad she stamped her foot and flew out of the window and sat in a tree!" Fredrick can barely catch his breath.

"Slow down, slow down. What was she so mad about?"

"Because guess what! Christopher and Stuart they marked up the whole floor. The whole floor! Even the blocks!"

"That sounds pretty awful, but I know Mrs. Paley didn't fly out of the window, Fredrick."

"She did, she did, I really saw her."

The children, in fact, have never seen me so angry. They will refer to the scene throughout the year as "the time Stuart and Christopher did the bad thing." Here is what happened: Stuart and Christopher, having spent most of the free play in a blanket-covered hideout, refuse to leave at cleanup time.

"Don't come in, don't come in," they call. "The chimney is closed you can't come in."

"You must come out, boys. We're having cleanup."

"No," is the faint reply.

"Sorry, boys, I'm taking away the blanket right now . . . oh lord! I can't believe this! What have you done? This is really awful."

My loud wail brings the entire class into the blocks. In shocked silence we survey the damage. A square yard of floor and half a dozen large blocks have been darkly scribbled upon by felt markers. Accustomed as we are to all sorts of "accidents," this is a truly bad thing.

"I can't believe you boys did this," I groan. Christopher

rubs his eyes and examines the red marker in his hand. "Stuart told me to do it," he mumbles.

"There is nothing more to say, boys. It's too big a job to waste time being mad. Who will help us? This might take the whole morning."

What follows surprises me more than the original event. Instantly, everyone rushes for rags and buckets. There is a great display of hard work and friendship.

"Look how I'm doing!"

"Watch my muscles, Christopher."

"I'm making my best job for you, Stuart!"

The atmosphere drips with more than soapy water; it is a tidal wave of relief and goodwill. The worst has happened and apparently no one is to be punished. The teacher was as angry as a stomping, flying witch, but the anger disappeared quickly and nothing bad happened to anyone.

The next morning, Fredrick can't wait to talk about it. "Remember when Christopher and Stuart did the bad thing?"

"I do remember. I'm still wondering why they did it."

"They thinked it was a fire."

"They were pretending it was a fire?"

"A *real* fire it was."

Later, in the music room:

"Some people are still talking about what happened yesterday. Fredrick thought you were making a fire, boys."

"We was burning up the wolf," Christopher replies quickly.

"But we've had pretend chimneys before and no one marked up the floor," I say.

"The wolf thinked this was real."

"He would know it's not real," Barney snaps. "A real fire hasta be from a fire you could burn yourself."

"Yeah, yeah, fire, fire, fire!" Fredrick jumps up and runs around the room aiming a pretend hose. "Fire! Wolf in the chimney! There, I got it out and I did *not* mark up the floor."

He returns to his seat, flushed and happy. Everyone nods in righteous agreement, staring at the unmarked rug.

Fredrick's way is better; even Christopher and Stuart see that.

Then why do the unthinkable? Perhaps nothing is unthinkable, and if no one is there to expose the myth of impending danger, the wolf can seem too real. A mother or baby would have been helpful; then the boys could have made beds or sat down to dinner. But none of these protective distractions were on hand to offset the destructive impulse.

The episode is still on Stuart's mind when, later, he pulls me away from the story table. "A bad thing! A bad thing! They're fighting!" he cries.

"I don't see any fighting, Stuart."

"Fredrick told them to get out."

"But look, they're all playing now, see?"

He stares in disbelief. Fredrick's angry words have connected to other angry words in Stuart's mind, stirring up images of combat that are hard to sort out. I'm certain he is thinking of his own bad thing because he keeps looking at the floor under Fredrick.

"Were you afraid they would fight?" I ask. "Did you think he might mark up the floor?"

"They really did fight. On the other day before this one."

"And they had to stop, remember? Because we only allow pretend fighting."

"Like this, right?" He cocks his finger and takes aim at Fredrick. "P-k-k! P-k-k!"

"Don't shoot at me, Stuart."

"I'm pretending."

"You do *not* shoot if someone says no," Fredrick announces in stentorian tones.

"Stuart was showing me how he pretend fights," I say. "Also, he was worried that you're angry at Barney and Christopher."

"Yeah, I am. They stealed my drinks."

"*He* took 'em from us!" Barney calls out. "And I'm making magic stuff that people can see it if they're my friend."

"I'm your friend," Fredrick says quickly.

"Me too," Stuart declares. "I'm your both friend."

Would that I could communicate my feelings so easily. I might have told Christopher and Stuart, "You're not coming to my birthday unless you clean up that mess." Then the limits of my anger would be perceived and Fredrick would not have seen me stamp my foot and fly into a tree.

13

The schoolteacher who studies and describes her own classroom cannot remove herself from the picture. A visiting researcher is free to focus on a specific behavior or child; I must try to see it all, and may need to deal with my own feelings even as I decide what to do about the child's. Or what to do about the child's view of *my* feelings.

Did Fredrick actually see me as a witch? If this could be so, even for an instant, then adult anger must be a fearsome burden for a child. When I bring up the matter, Fredrick becomes strangely distant.

"Mother told me you said I was so angry about the marked-up floor that I flew out of the window and sat in a tree."

Fredrick is startled but says nothing. Was I not to know? Is he surprised his mother knows?

"I could never do that, Fredrick, no matter how angry I was. I would never leave the room. And you know I don't punish people, do I?"

"No." He squints, trying to remember if this is so.

"I think it worries you when I'm angry."

"No."

Before I can respond, Mollie tapes a green square on Fredrick's shirt and begins to slither along the floor. "Pythons are green so we're green," she shouts. Immediately, Fredrick drops to the floor and follows her trail of green scraps.

"S-s-s. We're snakes. We need a snake hole," Fredrick hisses.

"We're not poison, Barney," Mollie says. "We need a few bunch of your blocks."

"No, Mollie. It's our hideout. Stop taking those, Fredrick," Barney warns.

"S-s-s. We're bad snakes. Poison blood. S-s-s. Mark up your hideout with poison blood. S-s-s."

"Don't, Fredrick! I'm telling! Stop!"

"S-s-s. We scared him away, Mollie."

"Bang, bang, bang!"

"Don't bang at me, Barney," Mollie says.

"I'm shooting at Fredrick, not you. He's the bad snake."

"Oh, yeah? I'll bite my poison on you."

"Not on me you can't." Christopher holds up a block. "I gots a sword to protect me."

"S-s-s. I eat swords and I can fly."

Mollie puts her hand on Fredrick's back. "Don't do it, little snake. Don't be a bad snake today because it might be your birthday."

"S-s-s. Pretend we scared him away, Mollie," Fredrick replies. "Pretend we're dangerous but people think we're nice."

"I'm the mother snake. S-s-s."

"I'm your baby, Mollie, and pretend I'm angry because I don't see you and then I can't find you and then I find you because your tail is showing and you tell me to come in the hole."

A poisonous, flying, sword-swallowing snake can mark up a hideout and threaten its inhabitants, and then instantly can become an angry baby demanding consolation from its mother. How easy, in play, to disguise the feelings represented by the actions. The more I listen, the more the play seems motivated by that which *cannot* be discussed.

Later, for example, Barney refuses to remember that he

called Jacques Cousteau a bad guy. He seems offended when I talk about it, though it was a crucial part of the drama I just observed.

"Trouble, trouble," he declares. "Jacques Cousteau!"

"Is that trouble?" Stuart asks.

"There *is* trouble, Stuart. Jacques Cousteau! Watch out! He's stealin' the gold!"

"Dinner's ready," Emily announces. "Yummy-yum."

"The bad guys are attacking the ship. Jacques Cousteau!" Barney looks out through a rolled up paper.

"Is he a bad guy?" Stuart asks. "Is Jacques Cousteau bad?"

"He's trying to break in here. Nine-one-one!"

"I'm making poisonous for you," Emily says. "Mix it up and give it to him."

"To who?" asks Barney.

"The bad guy you said. Jacques Cousteau."

"Wait, we need more gold. I'll be right back." Barney races to the table and begins tearing off bits of paper. "Dum-de-dum-dum. Pow!" His concentration is so fierce he does not hear my first question about Jacques Cousteau.

"Did I hear you say Jacques Cousteau is a bad guy?" I ask again.

"The sharks are."

"Not Jacques Cousteau?"

"He wasn't there."

"I heard his name . . ."

"That was a different name."

He gives me the same puzzled look he once gave a substitute teacher who asked him to stop doing something that was making her uncomfortable. When Barney is tired or preoccupied, he sucks his left thumb while rotating his right hand inside his shirt, bringing to mind a nursing baby. It is not meant to be seen by others, nor was Jacques Cousteau intended for my ears. I am also not to know that my anger turns me into a witch.

Even so, why *is* Jacques Cousteau a bad guy? The television series shows him and his associates studying, not fighting, the sharks. Or do the human swimmers appear to be the aggressors? More to the point of Barney's rules, however, since sharks are not to attack good guys, the Cousteau group must be given dual personalities. Bad guys attack and rob other bad guys. Why? Because if you are attacked, you *will* punish the attackers; those who punish—or who have the power to punish—are, to that extent, bad guys.

Thus, if my domain, the classroom, is attacked, I become the bad guy who will punish the wrongdoers. Even if no punishment follows, the *fear* of retribution is enough to change Cousteau into a sea monster and me into a witch. It also means that the event will be viewed in a variety of disguised situations.

"Pretend we're picking blueberries, Fredrick," Mollie says. "For your birthday pie that little snakes like."

"And then a witch sees us?"

"No witch, no witch."

"She doesn't see us but she hears our footprints."

"No witch, Fredrick. Not by blueberries. Not for good snakes."

"Not by the blueberries but she's taking a walk to see if someone is going to eat her house."

"Okay. Put some poisonous by the other place."

"Whoosh! No more witch that was scaring us. There was a witch scaring us, teacher," Fredrick tells me.

"What was the witch going to do?"

"Steal the mother."

Once Fredrick has a witch in mind, he must play a scene in which she is destroyed. As Barney has stated: You can't say no bad guys if you already said bad guys. We keep our disguises on until the danger is past.

14

What is the danger from which the children must continually escape? Is there one irreducible fear that underlies the others? It ought not be hard to discover, for the children are mere beginners in life. They have only recently been babies and, in many cases, already share the hearth with a new baby. They feel pleasure and pain; they know anger and have heard of death; they are in school, far from home. All this the children have in common.

In my search for the sources of fear, babies might seem the wrong place to begin; so often they present a nostalgic view of life before fear. Yet today, the girls act out a suprisingly scary explanation for new babies. This is not the usual "Pretend the baby just jumped out of the mommy," but a far deeper view of the subject.

Emily is the mother. She speaks to her daughters, Mollie and Margaret, in a strict voice. "Bedtime, sisters. Stay down and cover up. Something might happen."

"We know, mother," Mollie replies sweetly but Margaret is distracted. "Get out, Carrie!" she orders.

"Can I play with you, Mollie?" Carrie asks.

"Tell her no," urges Margaret.

"Let Carrie play, Margaret," I say. "She feels bad when you tell her to get out."

"But we need a time without Carrie."

"She has no one to play with. The others are outside. Now I want you to let her play. Who can she be?"

Mollie is willing. "She can be the other sister. But I don't know what pillow you can sleep on, Carrie."

"She can sleep on mine," Emily says.

Margaret is not happy, yet this very unhappiness initiates an immensely satisfying plot.

"A lion's going to eat you, Carrie," Margaret says.

"Why?"

"Because you're not under the blanket."

Emily responds immediately to the new story line. "Put your feet in, sister. A lion is coming."

"The lion will eat you up," Mollie says, "and then you'll be a new brand baby again. Just close your eyes, Carrie."

"Pretend that lion already ate me up. Pretend I'm a new baby right now."

"No, Carrie, first you have to be dead," Emily decides. "You're dead now. Carrie is dead, daughters. Bring her in the house."

"Where will she sleep?" Mollie asks, but Margaret is already preparing a bed. "In her own bed she sleeps. In Carrie's old bed because Carrie's dead for the new baby."

Do they really worry that the firstborn dies to make room for the new baby—or, rather, to *make* the new baby? The lion may have been called forth in response to Carrie's intrusion, but the girls all seem to recognize the new fantasy.

"Quick," Emily whispers. "The lion's going to eat Carrie the new baby up again. He's coming!"

"Then when she gets out she'll be a smaller new baby," Margaret says.

"Wa-ah, wa-ah," Carrie cries. "Pretend he ate me already. Now I'm the baby that stays and not another baby comes and no more lions."

"Okay, little new baby. We love you because you're new."

I think back to a kindergarten conversation in which Lisa, nearly six, described how mothers "get bones from dead dinosaurs and blood from a dead person" to make their babies. Every child in the class thought hers was a plausible explanation. Here are other girls, a year younger, acting out a similar theme with far more personal implications.

The next day, the story continues—without the lion. "I

wanna be the new baby today," Margaret says. "Pretend I was already alive. Now I'm no-old. This is my birthday not to be old, to be no-old."

"I'm your mother," Mollie tells her. "Pretend you said, 'Ca-ca-coo-coo-ma-ma.' "

"No, Mollie, I can't talk because no-olds can't talk anything. I just cry if I don't like anything."

"When do you learn baby talk?" Mollie asks.

"Never. Because I'm always no-old. I only cry." Margaret eyes Emily at the door. "Pretend I cry if sister takes my bed."

"Is there a sister?"

"There used to be. Then she got dead because pretend you're the mother and you only want one baby. Pretend I'm the only baby. If Emily plays she has to be the daddy."

"No," Emily argues. "I'm sixteen. That's a baby."

Later, I ask: "What did you mean, Emily, when you said 'Sixteen, that's a baby'?"

"That's how we play. When someone was sixteen pretend I'm the sister and I'm sixteen and then I'm a tiny baby going to get born."

"No-old," Margaret says.

I am vaguely disturbed by this line of thinking. "Girls, when it's not pretend, when it's real, you girls *know* you won't ever become babies again, don't you?"

"Yeah, we know," Margaret says. "But a new baby could come out, really, when nobody knows. Right, Mollie?"

Mollie nods. "And the mother eats and eats things you don't see."

"What do you mean!" Fredrick yells angrily. "The *dad* sees! My dad knows the whole thing because he even was there! That's how the baby got borned!" Fredrick looks so grim I feel I must say something quickly.

"I'm glad you told us about the new baby, Fredrick."

"I didn't say anything to you!"

15

Though it has taken Fredrick two weeks to mention the new baby, his sullen restlessness has already become a classroom fact. He paces the room, glowering, as if expecting a fight, and then sits for long periods at the story table, covering small papers with black crayon marks.

"Do you want to tell a story, Fredrick?"

"I hate stories."

"Well, if you change your mind . . ."

"All right, I changed my mind," he blurts out, beginning his story quickly.

> A baby cries and the mommy has to go get him. Then she has to snuggle him. Then He-Man tries to hurt the baby but he doesn't. Then He-Man has a fight with every bad guy.

He pushes his chair back noisily. "And *don't* ask me anymore! And don't ask me if I'm He-Man because I'm not! I'm always the baby from now on. And *don't* ask me!" He runs into the block area and lies down in a house Mollie has just built.

"This is my rainbow house," she says.

"Do you need a baby? I mean, I'm *not* the baby! I *am* the baby. Where's my bed? I'm crying and you have to snuggle me. You didn't bring me the blue blanket." He begins to cry.

"Are you really crying, Fredrick?" Mollie asks.

"No! Can't you just snuggle me, Mollie? Can't you bring me the blue one?"

"Here it is, little snuggle baby," Mollie murmurs. "Here's a nice beddy for you. Don't cry." She smooths his hair and covers him with the blue blanket.

"Mollie," Fredrick says calmly. "I'm the new borned person, okay? No father and no brother. Mommy and the baby. Don't let anyone come in, okay?"

Mollie begins to hum. "Mmm-mmm. No daddies—no baddies—mmm." She adds more blocks to the house while Fredrick moans and rocks under the blanket.

Fredrick sits beside me on the playground bench, his hand in mine. "Did you find out more about your mother's birthday, Fredrick? Did you ask your grandfather to tell her when it is?"

"I think he forgot."

"Now your family has another birthday to remember."

He is surprised. "What?"

"Your little brother will have one."

"Did he have a party that day he got borned?"

"I don't think so. But he *will* have a birthday party when he's one year old. By then, you'll be five."

"Mine always comes first, right?" He jumps down and kicks at a pile of tanbark. "That baby might live with the old man and the old woman."

"What old man and woman?"

"You know, teacher, they're lonely because they don't have any children?"

"Fredrick, are you thinking about the old man and old woman in *Millions of Cats*?"

"Did they want a baby or did they want a cat?" he asks with sudden urgency.

"She asks the old man to bring her a cat."

"Oh, I forgotted to say that's what I want." He climbs back on the bench and puts his head in my lap. "My grandfather is not old. He told me he's not an old man."

After a few moments, Fredrick joins Mollie in the sandbox. "This is my bed here, Mollie, so no troll could ever bother me. It's a trap. If somebody is a troll or somebody else bad I don't see them tries to push me out of this bed he falls in the trap and dies."

"What if it's a good person?" Mollie asks.
"Only a good mommy. Do you want to be that?"
"You mean snuggle?"
"And the mucky part."
"Okay, here's the mucky, little boy baby, just for you." She places her thumb in his mouth and rubs his back. It is a variation of Barney's nursing pantomine, and not for me to see or talk about. But Christopher, on a nearby ledge, sucks his own thumb and watches in deep concentration.

16

These are hard times for Fredrick, who now seems to find contentment only in the cradle. Luckily, he's in this group; last year, under Erik's leadership, it would not have been so easy for a four-year-old boy to persist in the role of newborn baby. Even so, Fredrick's demands are beginning to meet with resistance.

Though Barney loves Fredrick, he is not as tolerant as Mollie. "I'm king of the Boy Scouts," he says. "I can change into scary tigers. I'm a scary baby tiger."

When Fredrick hears "baby," he rushes into the block area. "I'm the baby tiger."

"You can be the daddy tiger," Barney tells him.

"No, you said baby."

Christopher tries to help. "Let him be the twin for the other baby, Barney. I'll be the dad."

"No twins!" Fredrick cries. "I'm the only baby."

Barney shrugs his shoulders. "Then who do I be?"

"You be the mommy for me," Fredrick says.

"No! I'm the baby tiger because I said it first. *You* be the mommy."

"I hate you guys! I said I was the baby and you won't let me. I hate you! I'm hating you every day from now on."

"What's wrong, Fredrick?" I ask.

"Nobody wants to play with me."

"Barney said you could be a twin baby tiger. That was a good idea."

"He's not my friend."

"Would you like to play with Petey and Jonathan?" I ask, pointing to several three-year-olds in the doll corner.

"Okay," he says tearfully, taking my hand. "You tell them to play with me."

"Hi, boys. Fredrick would like to play with you. Is that all right?"

"Yikes! The monster is here!" Petey shrieks.

"If I play I'm the baby kitty," Fredrick says.

"Superman!"

"Spiderman!"

"We're not playing that, you guys. I'm the baby kitty. You wanna be the mommy cat? Huh, Petey?"

"And could I beez the daddy?" Jonathan asks.

"No daddies. Just two mommies. I'm both of your baby cat. Meow, meow. I want my milk now." Fredrick lies down on the floor.

Petey smiles. "Mommy will come. Here, kitty, your bottle."

"I got chocolate milk for you, Battle Cat," Jonathan whispers. "Do you like that?"

"Don't call me that, Jonathan. Call me new baby, okay? Meow, meow. Put me to bed, two mommies. Don't go away."

The boys hug and pet Fredrick as they might a real kitty. "We won't go away, kitty, because we love you so much."

Fredrick squirms closer and the boys lower themselves gently on to his back. All three close their eyes and begin sucking their thumbs.

Mollie enters and watches the boys for a moment. "Do you want me to be your mom, little babies?" There is no response so she begins to set the table. "Sleepy, sleepy, sleepy, sleepy. I'll call you when breakfast is on the table. It's almost ready to go to school."

Later, Fredrick refuses Barney's invitation to play Cobra boat. Instead, he sits on the tractor a few feet away and stares past his friends as they skip from block to block trying to avoid "Lake Michigan ocean."

"Watch out, Fredrick. You're in Lake Michigan ocean. That's the deepest place where you are. Get on the Cobra boat."

"I'm busy," Fredrick says.

"Doing what?"

"Something."

"Watch out, it's deep water. You'll drown!"

"Yikes! It's wet everywhere." Christopher pushes more blocks together to make a platform. "Stand here, Cobra, you'll get wet. Hey, Cobra, let's attach our boats together. You and me are the captains." He glances at Fredrick, expecting to be challenged, but Fredrick is talking to himself, his back turned to the boys. "Fredrick, you know you're getting all wet," Christopher says, puzzled.

"You're sinking, Fredrick!" Barney howls.

"Never mind, I'll save you, Barn!" Christopher throws out a pillow. "Here's the life perverser!"

"We're both sinking, Christopher. There must be a leak. Fireman! Fireman! He can't sink. He can fly. Fireman!" Barney and Christopher run through the hallway, yelling "Fireman!"

Fredrick looks around, surprised to find the block area empty. Slowly he drives his tractor into the nearest wall of the Cobra boat and rolls back and forth until all the sides are down.

The sight of him in the rubble brings back an image of Fredrick at three knocking apart sand castles and spaceships to the consternation of his classmates. The word "water" comes to mind, and I smile recalling Fredrick's fledgling stories that contained but a single word: water. It had not been hard to dig out his secret.

"Did a bad thing happen in the lake?" I had asked.

"No."

"In a swimming pool?"

"Yeah. I drowned."

"Who pulled you out?"

"My sister. I went under again. And I went under again. And I went under again."

His mother was surprised: he'd been lifted out so quickly he hadn't even swallowed any water. It happened when he was two, she said, and he'd never talked about it before now.

"Fredrick, do you remember those water stories you used to tell? When you were three?"

"No."

"About falling in the pool and your sister pulled you out?"

"No."

"And then you decided to be the Incredible Hulk and you ran around saying, 'Hulk, Hulk, Incredible Hulk.'"

"Oh yeah! I *remember* that Hulk. And Erik let me be the Hulk, remember? And he made me a green thing on my arm, remember?"

"I do remember. You told a lot of Hulk stories last year." After his first Incredible Hulk story, in fact, he never mentioned the drowning episode again. It was one of those "moments of truth" for me; I hadn't yet realized the direct connection that could be established between a traumatic event and a superhero role. "Fredrick, I'll bet you told ten Hulk stories in a row."

"Oh yeah! And the Hulk jumped into the swimming pool and the lion tried to get me and I swimmed fast fast until I was home."

Fredrick goes off smiling and I am astonished. He has reconstructed almost verbatim a story of a year ago, yet the real life drama that spawned the story remains buried. Perhaps the new baby has brought back some of the same feelings: loss, helplessness, the sense of going under.

If there were to be a one-word story this time, it might be "baby." However, Fredrick invents another way to preserve his secret. He begins to tell stories in which he "hides" a sentence about the baby.

> Superman came. And He-Man came. And the mighty Gobots. The baby cries for his mommy. Then the bad robots come and they fighted Superman and they all die but Superman doesn't die.

When his story is acted out, Fredrick lies down in the middle of the rug. Superman, bad robots, and mighty Gobots play their roles around a curled-up baby who whimpers, "Ma-ma, ma-ma." No one asks why there is a baby in the story. They do not need to ask. It is the very stuff of which their fantasies are made.

17

"Fredrick's unhappy in school, isn't he?" his father asks. "He cries every morning and he doesn't want to get dressed."

"He *is* rather sad about the baby."

"Remember when he was three? He couldn't wait to come. He loved school."

"He'll love it again. I know he will."

"Should we keep him home for a while? That's what I really wanted to ask. He's so angry with us."

"I think he's better off in school, really. He's got his friends, he pretends to be the new baby . . ."

"He does that at home all the time."

"But here he can use substitutes for you and his mother. And besides, it fits quite nicely into the other children's play. Look, don't worry. It may take a while, but he'll work his way through it. Or, I should say, *play* his way through it."

The play is, in fact, quite unusual, even for school. It is so specifically focused on Fredrick's problem that the children give it a name: Watch out for the baby.

Throughout, the baby is indulged and protected while being subjected to one crisis after another. Each emergency seems intended to distract the mother away from the baby and then to reassure her that everything is under control. Fredrick is always the baby and speaks entirely in baby talk.

"Ma-ma. Appa ju. Appa ju."

"Baby wants apple juice, mother," Barney interprets. "Watch out for the baby. In case it's poison."

"Baby want banana?" asks Mollie.

"Don't give it to him," Christopher calls. "It might be poison. I fighted a bad guy that did it."

"Ba-gu-ba-gu-wa-ah."

Christopher wants Mollie's attention. "There really was a bad guy, mother. He was trying to steal your baby. I'm not kidding. Here's gold for a present."

Stuart will not be outdone. "This is the birthday cake, mother, for the baby. They gave you a new baby for a birthday present. It's your birthday, too."

"Ba-gu-ba-gu."

"Watch out for the baby," Christopher repeats. "I broke his bones off. Pretend I'm the brother and I broke his bones off. Not real."

"Yeah, pretend it's real," Barney urges. "The building is falling! Get out of the building, baby! I got to chop it down."

"Ba-ba-ba-ba."

"Don't cry, baby," Mollie says. "We love you."

"Fire! Don't let it get on the baby!" Barney yells.

"It won't. He's got on the magic vest. Nothing can ever hurt him."

"Wa-ah! Wa-ah!"

The play is frantic and noisy, but it is taken very seriously and follows a consistent script no matter how many children enter the story. Fredrick's infantile babble becomes louder and more persistent until it seems to dominate the entire classroom.

I decide to confront Fredrick with my growing

impatience. "You're pretending to be a baby a lot lately," I comment tersely.

He frowns and says nothing.

"I miss the other pretend people you used to be."

"Who?" He seems genuinely interested.

"Well, you were a pirate and a Boy Scout and . . ."

"I was the guard."

"How about playing that again?"

"I'm too tired."

"Maybe you . . ." but Fredrick is not listening. He stares at the doll corner waiting for someone to enter. As Barney and Margaret approach, he races ahead and jumps into a crib.

"Stay in your bed, baby. I'll cover you," Margaret says.

"Wa-ah. Bot-tee, bot-tee," Fredrick begins his chant.

This time Barney is annoyed. "Nobody needs to come in their bed, Fredrick, *every day,* you know. Because I can fight anybody, mommy. Get up, Fredrick, get up, guy. Guys! Fredrick! Get up. Morning time. You are *not* a baby, Fredrick!"

Fredrick's disappointment in Barney is evident. Perhaps *shock* is more accurate. "Ma-ma?" he says quietly.

"Hey, Fredrick, I see a bad guy. You wanna be on the bad guy team?"

"Ma-ma."

Barney drops to the floor. "I'm dead. Call a doctor. Fredrick, call a doctor. Emergency! Bad guys in the water. Get on board." He has pulled out every offering he can think of, and he turns to Christopher in dismay. "We gotta get away from here. Follow me, Christopher. We gotta do something! We gotta build something!" Finding the block area empty, he and Christopher blot out the crying baby in a frenzy of "real" work.

"Hammer that board!"

"Power saw. Br-r-r-r. Power saw!"

"Electric motor man! Put electric over there. Get all the tools, man. We need about a hundred."

Fredrick is happy to have Margaret to himself and kisses her hand gratefully. However, his pleasure is soon interrupted by Mollie and Emily.

"Who are you, Margaret?" Mollie asks.

"The mother."

"Let's be sisters," Mollie says. "We can put on all the dresses we want. I got the pink."

Margaret grabs the purple shawl. "Mine! I had it first, Emily!"

"Ma-ma, ma-ma."

"We're not playing baby, Fredrick," Margaret tells him abruptly.

"Ma-ma."

"Stop that, Fredrick," Mollie warns. "*No* babies. We didn't *have* our babies yet."

"Right," Emily agrees. "We're not sixteen yet. You can't play now, okay, Fredrick? No dad, no brothers, only sisters now."

"No fair, Margaret!" Fredrick explodes, jumping up and down on the bed. "You *never* play with me. I hate you. I *hate* you."

The girls ignore him, covering themselves with chiffon scarves and sequined vests. They begin to compliment one another extravagantly.

"Oh, how beautiful, sister."

"You are a gorgeous!"

"Say that I'm a beautiful princess."

"Here is a princess so beautiful in the woods. Pretend we're princesses and we don't know each other and all of a sudden . . ."

"All of a sudden you're stupid!" Fredrick stamps his foot like a wicked witch and swoops the dishes off the table. "Stupid babies!"

"Oh-oh. We're telling."

"Shut up!" He drags his pillow and blanket through the scattered dinnerware into the easel area and around the sand table, spreading sand and paint in his wake. By the time he reaches the blocks he is tear-stained and weary. He flops down next to the ship builders.

"This is my bed here, Barney. I'm the baby."

"No babies. *No* babies. We're builders."

"I can be one if I want."

"Then you can't play with us. Only if you're a builder. I'm . . . I'm He-Man builder. You can be He-Man worker. Okay?"

"Shut up, you guys. I'm not listening to you."

Christopher brings himself up tall. "I've got the lightning sword with all the power stuff, Fredrick. If I touch you, you'll die."

"Yeah," Barney adds, "this is a lightning rocket ship from when there's lightning."

"I'm never comin' back to this school," Fredrick says, dropping his pillow a few feet from the ship. He covers himself with the blanket until there is only a tuft of blond hair to reveal his identity. The ship builders continue to pound and blast, then suddenly become quiet, watching the blanket-covered form that lies motionless an arm's length away.

"Hey, that person is dead," Barney says. "Are you dead, Fredrick?"

"I'm sleeping."

"The poison lightning made you dead or asleep. You decide which. It's up to you."

There is a long silence, then, "I'm dead. If you see me dead, call the doctor," Fredrick whispers.

"Here's some firewood to make you alive."

"I'm just sleeping. Put the firewood because the boat is cold. Tell me when it's warm enough for me to take off the blanket so I come alive."

"Psh-sh. Psh-sh. Okay. It's warm by the firewood."

With a grand flourish, Fredrick throws his blanket aside. "I'm alive," he announces.

Were this the theater, Fredrick's woes would disappear now in a joyful finale, but "the real way" is never so simple.

Yet the social and dramatic forces at work in the classroom must inevitably exert their pull, and Fredrick begins to respond.

The next morning: Mollie has begun making the day's supply of pink hearts. "Hi, Fredrick. Do you need some pink hearts today?"

He picks out a heart and puts it in his overall pocket. "Hey, Mollie, you want to be a laser mom?"

"Is she a mother?"

"She's got real power *and* she's a mother too."

"Okay."

"And I got laser power also, mom. Pow! Pow! Laser power! I shoot a big laser power. I could fight anybody else. They don't kill us because we can turn into other powers."

"Am I the regular mother now?"

"Back to laser power! Back to mother! Here's your magic heart, mom. To shoot at them if they bother your baby. Uh . . . can I be the baby?"

18

Fredrick's preoccupation has affected everyone's play. Barney begins to bring his Care Bear to school, and a gentle mythology evolves that seems related to what Fredrick is doing but without the mother's role.

"It's better if you have mothers," Fredrick complains.

"We're all daddies," Barney insists. "Because don't you know Care Bears don't have mothers? Only they have daddies. Didn't you know that? Well, I know it."

Care Bears are popular this year but have not entered classroom fantasy play until now. Each pastel-colored bear comes with a name and function identified by means of a painted symbol. However, the children also invent their own labels, which they continually change as they act out the roles.

"I'm sunshine bear today," Barney starts off. "You could be the second sunshine bear, Christopher, or do you want to be sun*beam* bear?"

"I'll be funshine bear. Is he the baby?"

"No, the baby is nighttime bear. That's Stuart. You could be cousin bear or brave bear or . . . bee bear if you want to go 'buzz-buzz.' "

"Never mind, I'll be candy bear that eats whatever candy I want."

"Well, pretend I changed my name to nighttime bear," Barney says. "Call me blanket bear."

"Okay, Barn, me too. I'm baby blanket bear. You and me is." Christopher is his most affectionate when he has either Mollie or Barney to himself. "Night-night, my good pal nighttime baby blanket bear."

Mollie is also excited by the new Care Bear play, but Barney's exclusion of mothers confuses her. She sits now folding and taping a piece of orange paper into a small bumpy package. "Here you go, baby bear. It's your present, Barney."

"You mean I could keep that?"

"Keep it in your box until your birthday."

"Where's my box to keep it in?"

"In our Care Bear house! Put it where there's a little squeak hole. I'm the mother to tell you when your birthday is."

"We don't have a mother."

"Then I'm rainbow bear. She isn't a mother yet. Make the house taller, father, because Care Bears are small."

"Do we need magic, Barn?" Christopher asks. "Do Care Bears have magic?"

"I *got* the magic," Barney answers. "We need a place to hide."

"Because we saw pirates?"

"Because we got magic. Magic always needs a place to hide."

"I'm He-Man bear if there's magic," Christopher says.

"No. He-Man is too strong for Care Bear. They has to be

more quietly. They could have magic but they can't be so strong like that."

"Because they're really babies?" Mollie asks.

"Right. Babies could know magic sometimes."

Mollie now poses the question I might have asked myself: "If they are babies, why don't they have mothers?" Barney's logic is unassailable: "If you have magic, you don't need a mother."

Fredrick also searches for magic. He tells a new kind of baby story but it falls short of his expectations.

> A baby kangaroo comes. And then a monster throws him in a cage. The father kangaroo says, "Hey, Mr. Monster, I'll throw *you* in a cage." So he opens the door and the baby hopped out. But then the father tricked the monster and put him in a cage.

"That's such a good story, Fredrick."

"I changed my mind. I'm telling a different one."

"But the kangaroo story is really nice," I say.

He shakes his head. "It's not my really story. That's just a pretend one that I thinked about." His "really story" still has the hidden baby.

> One time He-Man came. The baby cries and the mother has to snuggle him. And He-Man kills all the bad guys.

"And you'll be the baby?"

"There isn't no baby . . . I didn't tell you . . ." The baby is becoming well hidden.

"It says here, 'The baby cries . . .'"

Fredrick stares at the paper. "Where is it says 'baby'?"

"Here. 'B-a-b-y.'"

Fredrick laughs. "Oh, that's a different story. I must have did two stories."

"Well, actually, Fredrick, you told three. Don't forget the baby kangaroo."

Fredrick whoops with glee. "Hey! I never telled so much in my turn. Did anyone else do that? Did Barney ever do that? Am I the only one?"

"I think you're the only one, Fredrick."

"Only one! I'm the only one!" He runs through the room waving his story papers, shouting "I'm the only one!"

19

Before the week is over, the Care Bear odyssey shows signs of strain. One problem, I think, is the confusion of roles. The attributes of the bears are too interchangeable: funtime bear and pirate bear are much the same as sunshine bear and funshine bear, none likely to arouse the sort of commitment that helps a memorable story develop.

Another problem may be the one suggested by Barney when he said, "He-Man is too strong for Care Bears." Since nothing bad happens in Care Bear land, you don't need powerful figures. However, if fantasy play is the stage on which bad things are auditioned, then Care Bear is destined for a rewriting job.

"Pretend this is Care Bear baseball house," Christopher proposes. "We have to rescue them, Barney."

"Rescue who?"

"The baseball pirates."

"Okay. Calling all Care Bears! Don't shoot anyone. Rescue the pirates!"

"Should I get some gold, Barn?"

"And take care of the sword too."

"Then you better change me into mighty Battle Cat." Christopher has begun to prowl between the rows of blocks. "Ahr-r-ah!"

"First I gotta change myself. By the powers! I'm He-Man! You're Battle Cat. Go-get-Mollie-ask-her-does-she-want-to-be-She-Ra."

"Who can I be?" Stuart asks.

"You can be the second He-Man brother. Bad danger in the night and in the day. Two He-Mans for the terriblest Skeletor he's so terrible nobody ever saw this before."

The boys drop to the floor, lunging and growling. The old adventures have sprung up to fill the need; now there will be threats to acknowledge and fears to overcome. Care Bear provided a necessary respite, akin to playing store or bank, but it could not contain the whole drama.

Yet, what if too much danger is exposed? When Fredrick continually hammers out the perils of a new baby, the children begin to pull away. He is not playing the danger game properly; the urgency of his message is too naked. In fantasy play, you sidestep that which cannot be controlled and devise scenes in which fears are resolved: the wolf in the chimney and the bad Cinderella are substitute hazards for life's real emergencies.

"Hey, Barn, which Care Bear are you?"

"I'm G.I. Joe. Who are you?"

"I'm Superman," Christopher replies. "That means we're both good guys."

Mollie is disappointed. "But didn't you see I brought bedtime bear? She's the mom."

"No can do, kiddo," Barney says, raising his arm in a salute. "Da-da! I'm the bad Superman. See if you can stop me, Christopher."

"With poison or kryptonite?"

"Both. Try to change me into the good Superman. Do it like this. Put your hands by your forehead. Hurry up. In one second I'm going to chop down the world."

"Not over here, Barney," Mollie warns. "This is the Care Bear cave."

"Whoosh! P-k-k-k!" Christopher takes care not to aim at Mollie. "P-k-k-k. All the bullets are on *you,* bad Superman!"

"Bullets can't hurt me. Use the sword."

Petey, who has joined Mollie in the cave, suddenly bounds up and begins to shoot Barney with a plastic banana. "Banana gun! Bam, bam. You bad guy! I got magic banana bullets. They could kill a bad Superman."

The boys stare at Petey. Such convincing stage business rarely emanates from the younger children. "How old are you, Petey?" Barney asks.

"Three."

"You wanna be a guard? To guard the castle?"

"Those guys want to fight me," Petey says.

"Sounds like trouble, guard. I'll help you. Dum-de-dum-dum. Pow!"

"I'll help you too, Petey," Christopher shouts. "Dum-de-dum-dum! Now we have to fly a very long time. Across the water. Watch out, they're shooting ray guns at us!"

Barney slumps to the floor, eyes shut tight. Petey rushes to his side, worried. "Did they kill you, Barney?"

"No." Barney picks himself up. "The only one that could kill you is God," he states.

"God?"

"Yeah, God. My brother told me that. He said they have a statue about that."

The fleeting memory of his brother's "real" explanation for death cuts through Barney's fantasy. He looks around the block area as if he has forgotten what he was doing; the context has been altered in ways he cannot understand. God belongs to the truly powerful grown-up world, and at this moment Barney feels disconnected to his own.

He walks to the bookshelf and extracts a large dinosaur book. The last time I read it to him he told me, "You know why I like dinosaurs so much? Because they used to be alive a long years ago but now they're just pretend."

"Would you like me to read you that book, Barney?" I ask.

He nods and brings it to me. "Just read the part about Tyrannosaurus Rex. He's the strongest in the universe. He was stronger even than God."

"Did your brother tell you that?"

"My brother doesn't know it. That was before my brother got borned. I think it was before God got borned."

Barney smiles to himself; he has figured out his own solution to the God problem. Some instinct prevents him from imagining himself to be God, but he can pretend to be Tyrannosaurus Rex, stronger even than God. He knows it is pretend, yet the feeling is not unlike climbing the ladder out of a trap.

20

Christopher often feels he is caught in a trap. Last year his fears were so pronounced it was hard for him to play with others unless Mollie was there to interpret words and actions for him. He no longer requires her mediation; however, he continues a comforting habit begun in the middle of the previous year: every day he finds time at school to act out a brief, solitary battle in which two opposing forces clash and his side wins.

Today he seems mesmerized by the task of snipping off bits of yellow paper and arranging them into two piles.

"I'm Leader One," he says. "Leader One, Leader One, cut-cut-cut-gold-gold-gold. Leader Two is trying to get my gold. Ha-ha! Cut-cut-cut. No, you don't. Or you'll die. I got the most gold to be rich. Ha-ha!"

His fingers sneak up and steal gold from Leader Two's pile. "I got your gold! Ha-ha! That means you're dead."

Fredrick also is playing alone. He glides past Christopher, peering down at him through narrow eyes. "He-Man," he whispers, showering an unaware Christopher with a noiseless battery of bullets. "He-Man," he repeats at the easel, exchanging his invisible guns for paintbrushes. "He-Man," he says again with each slash of paint until the paper is mud-colored.

Mollie and Margaret, at the sand table, seem oblivious to He-Man and Leader One, yet a piece of each boy's fantasy enters their own.

"Smooth it down," Mollie says.

"You blobbed my cupcake down," Margaret responds.

"Say that to your brother, Margaret."

"Okay, I'll say it when I get home. Hey, Mollie, this is a grabbing mountain. Say 'grabbing mountain.'"

"Grabbing mountain."

"Now listen, Mollie. When it gets bigger you have to put a smile on it and two big eyes and a nose so people will think it's nice and they'll make a hole and say, 'Try to get out.' It's a trap. A trap will fall and cover them all up. Say 'bad mountain.'"

"Bad mountain."

With each handful of sand, Margaret grows more animated. She and Mollie often played "Copy what I say" when they were three, but it went little beyond simple mimicry. At four the plot has thickened.

"It *is* a bad mountain, Mollie. For *real*. The evil spirits go in here and capture the gold. The good spirits will be trapped in here forever."

Mollie is enchanted by Margaret's imagery. "Should I tap down the bad spirits?"

"Pretend my brother is in there. Watch out, he's getting out! The people are getting out, Mollie! Make it stronger. If they think to call He-Man he can't hear them."

"My sister is in there, too," Mollie says quietly.

The illusion of power is reassuring. Leader One captures the gold; He-Man moves invisibly through the room; the bad mountain silences all the people, especially younger siblings. One can feel safe and strong inside a disguise, but it is quite another matter, as Margaret often discovers, to demand bare-faced power offstage.

"Get out, Stuart!" she screams later in the doll corner.

"I don't have to."

"Yes, you do. I'm playing with Christopher. Get out before I hurt you." She gives him a mean look.

"I'm telling," he says, leaving.

"Good, he's gone. I hate him, don't you? Sit here, Christopher. Hold this baby."

"I don't want that doll in my lap."

"Yes, listen to me! You have to! Because I already have the other baby in my lap, Christopher. Listen to me! Listen!"

"That hurts my ears, Margaret. I'm going to play with Stuart."

"You're stupid! I hate you, stupid boy."

"I am not."

Christopher finds Stuart stretched out in a partially assembled block structure. "Y'wanna be guards?" he asks, and the boys quickly erase Margaret's anger with the authority of their official positions. "You look for trouble, Stuart. I'll make the trap."

Why is Margaret so angry, I wonder. Do her dark moods have their roots in the same quicksand that holds fast to Fredrick? I enter the doll corner and sit beside her. "You're all alone in here," I say.

"Nobody is playing with me."

"Shall I help you find someone to play with? Or would you like to tell a story? I'm not busy."

Her face brightens. "A story. I'm already telling one in my head." As we walk to the story table I begin to imagine the story she will dictate: bad mountains and evil spirits demolishing the world.

I am wrong. The power of fantasy to invent new ways to release one from a trap must never be underestimated. Margaret's story transforms her instantly into the nicest little girl in the whole world, someone who knows how to make a bunny happy.

> One day a bunny was planting a carrot patch for herself. Then a nice little girl the nicest little girl in the whole world comes and the nicest little girl says, "If only you give me those seeds, I will help you plant the carrot patch." Then the

> bunny said, "If I only give the seeds to the little girl, she will plant them for me." So she gave the seeds to the nicest little girl. Then one day they had a big carrot garden and the bunny was happy.

"Mollie, come to the sand table," Margaret calls. "I want to do what we did before. I'm making the bad mountain much badder."

"I'm busy," Mollie replies.

"Then I'm not your friend."

Mollie is vexed. "You still have to be people's friend even if they're busy."

"Well, aren't you coming?"

"I *am* going to come but right now I'm very busy, don't you see?"

"Then you're never coming to my house."

"Margaret!"

"Don't yell, Mollie. Okay, you could come. But who will do all the work here? It's already starting to get a big mountain. Don't you want to trap the people like before, Mollie? Wasn't that fun? Mollie, don't you want to trap my brother?"

"All right, here I come." She skips to the sand table. "La-la, you blobbed my cupcake down."

"Say that again, Mollie. Say everything I say. You blobbed my cupcake down. Say that. Then you'll be my best friend even in heaven."

"You blobbed my cupcake down. Hey, Christopher! Come here. We got a great trap."

Margaret is shocked. "No, Mollie, don't call *him*. Just me and you. Pretend you only see me. There isn't any more people. Will you do that, Mollie? Please, Mollie?"

21

"You never play no more with me," Fredrick complains to Mollie soon after Margaret's outpouring.

"I'll make myself some hearts and I'll give you one," she replies.

"But why won't you play with me?"

"I do sometimes."

"Not baby you don't."

"Would you like to be Starlite? Do you want to play the memory game? Y'wanna make something in the blocks?" Mollie continues to cut out hearts while she names some of her favorite activities. "Should we paint? Do you want to build a sand castle?"

"No, no, no." Fredrick wanders off listlessly, pausing in front of Petey's block structure. "That's not a good building, Petey," he observes.

"I'm a cash register man," Petey says. "You could be one. You wanna?"

"Where's the food?"

"This is the drinks." He points to a row of wooden cylinders.

"Those aren't drinks." Fredrick swings his arm and knocks them down. "I spilled all your drinks."

"Why?" Petey is more curious than angry.

"Because I'm making a hideout, that's why."

"Can I come in it?" Petey asks.

"No one can come in. It's a disguise hideout that no one can see. I need some of your blocks, okay, Petey?"

Petey is not one to hold grudges. In fact, he seems eager to contribute blocks to the new project. Fredrick puts up the four walls quickly, leaving himself a small entrance. "Get me the blue blanket, Petey. Hurry up. And don't tell anyone who's in here. And don't say my name."

Petey complies with Fredrick's requests, then sits quietly watching the covered hideout. "Who's in there?" Barney asks him.

"It's not Fredrick."

"Can I come in, Fredrick?" Barney shouts through a crack.

"No."

"Why not?"

"I'm not in here."

Barney frowns. "Fredrick is selfish," he tells me.

"He wants to play alone," I say.

"That means he's selfish."

"I'm not selfish. I'm hiding."

Barney looks interested. "You want a secret knock?"

"Tell me."

"It's a secret."

"Okay. Come in."

As soon as he arrives the next day, Fredrick builds his hideout again, but every few moments he emerges to get something: crayons, scissors, a book about trucks, two small racing cars. Finally, he brings in a telephone and starts making calls.

"Hello, hello? Is the baby crying? Oh, well, just let him sleep until he wakes up. Hello, hello? I'm doing work. Here's my number. Six-two-twenty-two. Call me to leave me a message."

For the next ten minutes, Fredrick talks on the telephone, scribbling messages and taping them to the blocks. Suddenly he springs up, knocking over two walls as he leaves. He gallops into the doll corner, pushes Raggedy Ann out of her crib, and falls heavily onto its pillowy center. Emily and Mollie smile distantly and continue dressing a Barbie doll.

"Mommy, can I dress up the baby?" Emily asks. "She's going to a party."

"She wants to stay home, sister," Mollie says. "She's playing in her bed."

"Pretend it's a nighttime party. For my babies."

"But I'm the mother, Emily, so I have to lullaby the baby. Give her to me, please." Mollie wraps the Barbie doll in a blanket and sings sweetly.

"Sh-sh baby sleepy go to sleepy are you asleep or are you silly? Little wind blowing see how I blow. Do you see me or do you want anything I have? Mmm will you sleep mmm oh sleep oh sleep mmm to sleep good little baby I love you sweetheart."

Fredrick sits up, smiling broadly. "You're a good mother, Mollie," he says on his way out of the doll corner. "Hi there, Barney! What's new, Mr. Blue? Hi there, teach! Hey, teach, you want me to paint something nice for you?"

"Yes, I'd like that."

"I was just now playing with Mollie."

"Were you the baby?"

"I wasn't even a person. I was a rester."

There is something about a cheerful greeting and smiling face that gives one hope. If Mollie's joyful lullaby reminded Fredrick of good feelings from the past, it is because he is ready to listen to the melody.

22

It is the old Fredrick who enters this morning waving a teddy bear and speaking of new plans and procedures. "Hey, Mollie, y'wanna see my bear? I'm building him a house big enough for him to sit or lay down. See this football shirt he's wearing? I weared it when I was a baby." He looks around, surprised. "Where is everyone?"

Mollie and I are covering the painting table with newspaper. "You're early, Fredrick. Mollie always comes to school before the others."

"Why do you, Mollie?"

"Because Mommy goes to work first before Daddy goes

to work second and Daddy makes breakfast for Leslie and then Mrs. Manly comes and Daddy goes to work second."

"Oh. But if your mother has a new baby then *she* goes to work second, right? Hey, get the blue blanket for the bear's house. Afterwards we're going to build *our* house. The parents do *not* live with his child."

His words grow more emphatic with each directive. "Hand me the small blocks, not the big ones, Mollie." He intends to be in full command of his bear's destiny.

"If the bear wants to write he needs these," Mollie says, her arms loaded with crayons and paper.

"He's too little for writing, Mollie. Don't bring that in his house. But when he gets bigger he's going to yell out and then we'll give it to him."

Fredrick seems himself again and Mollie acts as if he has never been anyone else. Was I the only one whose expectations were not met? The children use a far different scale with which to judge one another; they are more perplexed when someone refuses to evacuate an area designated as "Lake Michigan ocean" than if the same person chooses to lie in a crib for several weeks. Fredrick's extended infant role may have annoyed his classmates after a while but it did not appear illogical.

Nor does it seem odd to Mollie or Christopher, who is next to arrive, that Fredrick has changed overnight from baby to leader. "Can I play with you guys?" Christopher asks. "Can I, Fredrick?"

"It's up to Mollie," Fredrick tells him. "You can play if you ask her." The handing over of authority is a means of announcing one's own control. Barney often does this, and Mollie uses the politeness code to achieve the same ends.

"You have to ask *us* if you want to build," she says primly. "You have to ask *people* or it won't be polite."

All this is prelude to the story itself, preliminary procedures that set the stage. As Fredrick reenters the social scene on a more ordinary basis, he savors the sounds of a sturdy, dependable framework.

"We both got green alligators, Christopher," he says, pointing to the emblems on their shirts. "Everyone whoever gots a green alligator stand by me." Christopher moves quickly to his side. "There. Now, listen to me. Don't shoot over there. *Don't*."

"Why?"

"That is our *bear*. Don't. It'll make him die. And go right now and make this house higher. If anyone shoots bullets they go over his head. And *also*, by the *way*, don't make the sides so they might fall down because the bear will be hurt if you do that. So *don't*."

Having set forth some important do's and don't's, Fredrick is ready to introduce the characters.

"Now this is football bear. He lives in a little forest house that no one bad can see it."

"With blueberries all around," Mollie says.

"So they'll think he's nice." Christopher completes her thought.

"I'm the father that brings him presents," says Fredrick. "Pretend I almost gave him one but there was a hole and I fall in and drop the present but then I climb out."

"Here's the ladder," Christopher says. "Battle Cat! I'll get the present, master, because I got the sharp claws for that."

"He-Man! By the power of Grayskull! I changed you into Battle Cat. Get-the-present-in-the-hole!" The boys seem to be losing the original story, but Mollie is not distracted.

"Happy birthday to you, little baby bear. Oh, I'm so glad to see you born today."

"Don't step there, mother." Fredrick takes Mollie's hand. "It's still the trap. You have to pick blueberries from the other side."

"I got all we need, father. Here's the pie for the baby's birthday."

Fredrick observes Mollie with mixed feelings as she changes his bear into a baby, covering it with the blue blanket and humming one of her lullabies. He paces back and forth; his initial rhythm has hit a snag.

"Rock to sleep when the wind blows sh-sh-sh the cradle falls down I pick up the baby sh-sh-sh all goes to sleep again."

"Hey, mother, I think some bad guys might hurt your baby," Fredrick advises.

"Sh-sh-sh rock to bye the baby."

"Should I call the police?" he asks in a quieter voice.

"Sh-sh. The baby is asleep."

"That's not a real baby, you know. We could talk loud."

"Sh-sh. Baby is sleeping, sleeping."

Fredrick stops circling the room. "I'll be right back, mother. I have to hunt for a lion. For our supper. The baby is hungry for lion meat." He runs to me at the story table. "Hurry, teacher, I need a cape. I need one for hunting. The dad is a hunter. Hurry up, because there might be a lion in the forest."

The sobbing infant is gone, removed to some deeper recess, and the hunter takes its place. A master of disguise, Fredrick will conjure up new dangers and, with a flick of his cape, be the instrument of rescue. In so doing it is he who is saved.

23

I must not presume too much; only small segments of the drama are revealed to outsiders. Perhaps I exaggerate expectations of danger because this part of the plot is accompanied by such excitement and tumult. Yet the fantasy play is filled with warnings, and the children continually find new ways to describe the risks in life.

Mollie, Emily, and Margaret, for example, act out a scene that could be called "The Angry Mother." It hinges on the words "tired" and "messy."

"I hate this dolly, mother," Emily says. "Don't you? She

makes the table so messy. She has no mother anymore. You can't have a mother if you're so messy, right?"

"Just look at this mess!" Margaret shouts. "Clean up this mess! Listen to me. You're making me too tired."

"Don't be tired, mother," Mollie says. "I'll clean it up."

"Pretend the dolly keeps messing up and you don't like her," Emily urges.

"Put her in bed. I'm too tired. Sh-sh. She's sleeping. If you wake her up she'll mess up again."

"She's up, she's up! She's messing up!" Emily and Mollie begin to throw pieces of playdough on the floor and Margaret stamps her foot. "Look what you did, baby. Go to your room. Lock the door. I'm too tired."

"Don't be tired, mom. We baked you a cake. It's your birthday so the baby is good now."

"Should the baby do some more messy?" Emily asks.

Mollie shakes her head and looks about uncertainly. "Don't," she says. "Because what if the teacher thinks this is school?"

No wonder Mollie is confused. The girls have followed the logic of *their* curriculum, pretending the baby is bad in order to have it lose and then regain the mother's love. Nonetheless, Mollie suspects that, according to the rules of *my* curriculum, their behavior may be open to question. Oddly enough, I sound to myself exactly like the angry mother. We may be replaying the same scenario.

"Girls, girls, look at this mess. It's everywhere. Look at your shoes. Oh, my. Look at the beds."

"No, it wasn't the sisters," Mollie begins. "It was the . . . the baby did it."

"The doll?"

"I mean we pretended . . . the doll pretended . . ."

"Why couldn't you pretend to be the sisters who clean it up?"

"We *did* pretend," Emily says.

"Wait." I pause. "I'm getting mixed up myself now. I mean, I wish you could *pretend* the mess. Not have a real mess."

"We will," they answer, with great sincerity. But next time the mess will happen in the same way. How else can a pretend mother become pretend angry? If the angry mother role is to be acted out, then the anger and the mess must look real.

Moments after I leave a cleaned-up doll corner another drama begins. Barney, Fredrick, and Christopher enter on all fours, characters looking for trouble. But the girls have already acted out *their* bad thing and have no need to respond in kind.

"Gr-r-r! Trouble, He-Man, look. Strange people in here." Barney crawls up to each girl and growls at her. The girls smile back.

"Ah-r-r! Trouble coming!" Christopher roars, and Mollie pats his head affectionately.

"Hey, Mollie, a bad rabbit is outside tyring to get in," Fredrick says. "You better hide," he snarls, clawing the air. "Bad rabbits. Calling all bad rabbits!"

"Once I saw a bunny at the zoo," Mollie says. "You want to pretend this is the zoo? Come under here. Here's good carrots for you, rabbits."

"Can I play with you, Mollie?" Christopher asks. He appears to be already playing with her, since she is feeding him a carrot, but apparently he needs to be singled out in some way, given a special role, if he is to stop being Battle Cat. "Do you want me to be baby Battle Cat or something else?"

Barney is displeased by the sudden turn of events and steps out of character altogether. "Who knows something? Soon we'll be in kindergarten. Do you know that? *Kindergarten.*"

He has grabbed the spotlight. "Which day are we going, Barney?" Mollie asks, dropping her carrot and standing up.

"I don't know," Barney admits.

"But is it a long day from now on?"

"I don't remember which day."

"It's Friday," Fredrick says. "Teacher, are we going to kindergarten what Friday from now?"

"On a Friday that's after the summer. Next September. You still have a long time to be in nursery school."

The children are visibly relieved. Fredrick smacks Christopher playfully and they begin chasing each other, yelling "Nursery school! Nursery school! Get the kindergarten!" Any unknown, it seems, can be made into a bad guy.

24

I used to think Battle Cat was a bad guy; I know him only through watching the children play. He is the one that timid Cringer becomes when there is trouble. Actually Battle Cat is He-Man's pet and friend, most assuredly a good guy. I was fooled because the girls don't invite him to birthday parties. They say he is too wild.

Figuring out who is good and bad in fantasy play is usually easy, but in books it is quite another matter; the children and I are often far apart in our analysis of character and plot. This comes across with startling clarity when Barney makes an ordinary little boy from a Chinese folktale into a bad guy. The girls see his point instantly, but I need an explanation.

Margaret and Emily have been having an intense argument that does not yield to my logic: "She's not the mother!" Emily screams. "I was here first."

"No! I opened the oven first so I'm the mother!" Margaret yells back. "Take your hands away. *Stop,* Emily!"

"Don't push her, Margaret. Both of you can be mothers."

"Only me," Margaret whines. "I had the oven first. She hasta be the sister."

Barney, observing the scene from the telephone table, calls out, "Message from bad guy! Watch out!"

"Where is he?" Margaret asks.

"In the well. Remember?"

"Oh, yeah. Keep him there so he'll be stuck," Emily says. "Should he stay in the well, Barney?"

"I killed him. Don't worry."

"Oh, good, now we can cook him for supper."

When Barney leaves the doll corner, I ask him about the bad guy in the well. "Who was he?"

"That's from *Tikki Tikki Tembo*."

"The boy who falls in the well?"

"He's a bad guy."

"The little boy? How can he be a bad guy?"

Barney is surprised that I don't know why. "Because the mother is more sadder when *he* falls in, don't you remember?"

That aspect of the story had escaped me. Two brothers fall into a well at different times and the mother does in fact seem more concerned about the fate of the oldest whom she calls "best beloved." His name, in Chinese, is so long that the younger son has difficulty reporting the accident, a situation that is supposed to be the humorous focus of the story. However, for Barney and the others, the central fact lies in the mother's stated preference for her oldest child.

If you fear that you may not yourself be best beloved, you do not wish to be told such a possibility exists. No wonder Barney's literary reference rechannels the girls' anger, whereas my suggestion to increase the number of mothers is of no help. What if I had said, "Pretend you are sisters and you don't have a mother"?

Later I do try to promote an alternate fantasy during a dispute, but without Barney's success. A small group has been monopolizing the big blocks, refusing to allow anyone else to enter their house. "There's no room," they keep repeating.

"That's what the ant said in *Mushroom in the Rain*," I say eagerly. "But then each time he lets one of the animals come under the mushroom, it grows larger. How about if you do the same? Come on, I'll help you." The children listen to my plan with great interest, then begin to disperse to other occupations. Unaccountably, the play is over.

That my morality tale has disrupted the play should come as no surprise; I did not even bother to find out what the children were playing. Perhaps they were in a hideout, waiting for bad guys, or on a ship surrounded by sharks. Under such circumstances my analogy would make no sense.

Barney's bad guy in the well was altogether in context. The image of an unfair mother who loves one child best supports the girls' angry feelings of the moment. My motherless sisters idea might have worked also. When fantasy is the medium, compromises are easier to find, notwithstanding my poor choice of *Mushroom in the Rain*.

Conversely, the young child who is not pretending can be quite inflexible. If Christopher cries at music time because the seats on either side of Barney are taken, it does no good to promise him a turn the next day; for him, there is no tomorrow, only *now*.

The issue seems to exist, in fact, between the child and the adult, since every other child identifies immediately with Christopher's need. It is the teacher who wishes the matter settled quickly so that she can get on with the activity.

In play, however, the principle of compromise begins to represent a higher order of behavior to the children themselves. Christopher has a number of options under his control. He can change Barney into Battle Cat, get on his back, and race away. Or, if nothing else of an intimate nature can be worked out, he can at least guard the castle and be on the lookout for trouble. Every compromise advances the plot, and the players are grateful.

25

The children's talk flows past at a rapid rate. Given my self-imposed role of drama critic, I am bound to track down as many loose threads as possible. Yet these actors in covered hideouts may not be intruded upon too often. If called upon to deal with an emergency, I am then part of the plot, but I must resist most other on-the-spot inquiries or risk ending the drama.

Sometimes, as in the case of the bad guy in the well, important connections are clarified afterwards, a necessary reminder that random play only *seems* so because I haven't figured out the immediate—or distant—line of association.

The children do not require such reminders. They assume their behavior connects to everyone and everything else, and they will, if allowed, pursue an action until a connection is made. This need to establish relevance can involve a simple wordplay or absorb an entire morning's activity.

"Twinkle toes," says Margaret.

"Twinkle bows," Emily responds.

"Twinkle toesies."

"Twinkle bowsies."

"I'm Twinkle Toes and you're Twinkle Bows, okay, Emily? Pretend we're sisters."

More often, however, Margaret sees things in defensive terms. Today she arrives early with an empty medicine bottle in her hand and a scowl on her face, which intensifes the moment she sees Barney and Mollie playing together. How will she manage to connect her sour mood and her medicine bottle to Mollie's play?

"Blast me down, you silly medicine. Mollie, I'm going to blow up the whole earth," she begins.

"We're playing Rainbow Brite, Margaret."

"Watch out, Mollie, this is dangerous!"

"I'm not doing that, Margaret. Come here, Starlite. Here's the menu. Put a mark with your hoof if you want a thing to order." Barney neighs and stamps his foot.

"This is really dangerous, Barney," Margaret continues. "If you stamp too loud it'll blast you off. Water, then powder."

Barney pays no attention to the interruption. "Here, Rainbow, count this money for the restaurant. Hide it under here."

"You want to hide it under the blasting powder?" Margaret shakes the bottle an inch away from Barney's nose. "Hey, you guys, if I spill this stuff the whole world will blow up."

Mollie pushes the bottle out of the way and climbs on Barney's back. "I buyed you a toy, Starlite. I'll put it in your cabinet and lock it up so Lurky doesn't find it."

"Oh, Lurky. Lurky!" Margaret shouts. "Oh, did I tell you? I just blew him up with my blasting powder."

"Good, Margaret, get rid of Lurky. Did you kill him?" Barney asks.

"Yeah, I did. I'm the blasting powder guard, okay?"

"We'll call you Mellow Yellow and also the blasting powder person," Mollie says, looking directly at Margaret for the first time.

"Are you my friend, Mollie?" Margaret asks.

"Yes, I am."

Was the blasting powder really necessary to get Mollie to play with her? The intrusions seem counterproductive. Yet Margaret listens carefully, waiting for an opening. With the mention of Lurky, her explosive impulses find an acceptable outlet.

The ease with which Margaret linked her fantasy to Mollie's on this day cannot be guaranteed every time. Had she struck a discordant note—Barney might have wanted Mollie's total attention—there would have been too many bad feelings exposed for a simple conclusion. If, in addition, the teacher walks in with more unharmonious demands, the scene can fail miserably, leaving everyone unprotected.

This is what happens the next day, and my frustration equals the children's. The sounds of crashing pots and high-pitched squeals bring me rushing into the doll corner. Christopher, precariously balanced on the refrigerator, is throwing plastic fruit and playdough at Barney and Fredrick, who crouch under the table. "Ha-ha! Gotcha! Poop in your pantsers!"

"You missed, you missed, butt-face!"

"Gotcha, gotcha, poop in your pantsers!" Christopher is red-faced and breathless.

"Come down, this instant, Christopher. What do you think you're doing? This is not allowed in school."

He is too excited to pull back. "It's doll-corner smashie."

"What is *that* supposed to be?" My question is not the sort that initiates a discussion.

"It goes smashie-poopie-smashie."

"Look, all of you. Just pick everything up right now. And put all those chairs back."

The boys are suddenly unified in opposition to me. "But that's our place to sleep. We *made* it!"

"No. It's too messy. People could fall." I turn to leave, not offering to help, and Christopher runs to the telephone table.

"I'm going to call the police on you," he says. "I'm calling the police on the *teacher*."

"Yeah, call the police on her," Fredrick says.

Barney gives me a guilty look. "They're calling the police on you."

Christopher dials furiously. "We're calling the police to put you in jail. Police! Get angry at her. Put her in jail!"

I am startled at the pain I experience. Calling the police to put a classmate—by name, not in disguise—in jail always provokes tears and rage. Now I know the sensation; it is not the threat but the anger behind it that is so frightening.

I respond quietly. "I'm glad I'm not playing with you boys, because then I would really be upset. Now let's just clean up the mess together so people can play in here."

There is a sudden hush. The joyful camaraderie that accompanied the floor-marking cleanup is missing from our gloomy group. We have all been caught unguarded. But how strange that I should act in so fragile a manner. From some deep well of my own memories come feelings too powerful to ignore or disguise: fears of rejection, of being not best loved.

As I transcribe the day's events, my index finger, unbidden by me, it seems, flips swiftly past the jailing sequence. Clearly, I do not wish to hear a replay of the children's anger. I wait a day, then retrace the events made permanent on the tape. Nothing has changed for me: it still hurts to write it down.

26

The next day I am bound to make amends, but the boys act as if nothing has happened. "I'm sorry we got so upset yesterday," I say, cornering them in the blocks. Their puzzlement seems genuine, but I cannot let the matter rest. "I'm talking about how angry I was when you were throwing stuff in the doll corner."

There still is no response; the boys squirm and look away. "And you were so angry," I continue, "you called . . . you *pretended* to call the police to put me in jail."

All three stare at me in surprise. "Not a *teacher* put in jail," Fredrick says. "*Never* a teacher."

"Not for a teacher, no," Christopher agrees. "For bad guys. He was hiding under the table, remember, you guys?"

"Yeah, yeah, he was trying to come to our picnic and we moved everything to fool where we was," Barney says excitedly. "We hit him with the banana bomb and the pear bomb, oh boy!" The boys giggle with pleasure at the thought of events that took place before I walked in. My involvement has disappeared as mysteriously as the witch in the tree.

Their fantasies protect them against anger, theirs and mine. If the first fiction they create proves too threatening, there is another ready to take its place. They give themselves as many chances as they need to emerge safely from the trap, as in Fredrick's story.

> Once He-Man came. Then he falls in a trap where he wasn't looking. Then he climbs out because there was a ladder. Then he fights a bad guy by the outside of the trap and the bad guy falls in. But the good guy says, "That's not a trap for me."

"Why didn't the bad guy use the ladder to climb out?" I ask.

"No, it was a trick. It wasn't really a ladder."

"But He-Man used it."

"That's how come it's a trick." Fredrick laughs. "It tricks the bad guy. Bad guys can't *have* ladders." He runs over to Barney. "Hey, Barn, remember that trick we did in the sand table about the ladder? I just told it to the teacher."

Today the play is subdued; bad days often have a sobering effect. Injunctions hastily arrived at during a crisis are seldom needed the next day. Magically, problems are gotten rid of in the course of creating them. The anger, the explosion, and the guilt clear the air for new beginnings.

"If you want to play, boys, you have to be my horsies," Mollie says. "I made you a lovely barn for you."

"I'm baby Starlite," Barney decides. "Who are you, Christopher?"

"Second Starlite."

"Fredrick could be third Starlite or the dad," Mollie says.

"I'll be the father. Pretend I'm running away, Rainbow. Pretend I'm a dad who runs away."

"Don't you rather be a good horsie?"

"First we'll be good," Christopher answers, "and then we'll run away."

"But don't be so long, horsies," Mollie calls out after the boys, "because you can get out and run away or if you don't want to run away then you have to be quiet."

Fredrick bucks and whinnies, then grows calm. "Are you going to marry me, Rainbow?" he asks. "I'm brother Starlite."

"I'll marry brother Starlite first and then I'll marry baby Starlite and then second Starlite."

"But you know, Mollie," Fredrick responds slowly, as if to make certain the thought comes out just right. "Brothers are the strongest horses. A brother is stronger than a dad because he's also a brother and also a dad."

I know exactly what Fredrick means and cannot resist telling him so. "I think I see how you figured that out, Fredrick. You are a brother now and when you grow up you'll be a dad. So you'll be . . . as strong as both together, a brother *and* a dad."

Fredrick looks at me proudly. "That *is* what I figured out," he says. I blush with gratitude.

27

The rhythm flows in both directions: an overload of Rainbow Brite leads to dramas with higher peaks and more dangerous curves. The boys are more likely to tire of tranquillity sooner, but this time it is the girls who produce a sharp change in content and mood.

Emily has seen a television program that confuses and worries her. The terrain is unfamiliar, the fears so strange they cannot be disguised. Yet, in three consecutive days of acting out the unknown, the girls find a means of taking control: *they invent the bad guy*.

First Day

EMILY: Do you want to have boyfriends?
MOLLIE: Are we sisters?
EMILY: My boyfriend Derek is coming to kiss me. Do you want to play that?
MARGARET: Can I do that too?
EMILY: What's your boyfriend's name?
MARGARET: I don't know. Tell me what.
EMILY: Do you want Derek or Steven?
MARGARET: Derek or Steven.
EMILY: Okay, Derek. He's coming to kiss you on your body.
MARGARET: Only on my cheek. Not on my body.
EMILY: Then you can't have it. That's not sexy. Only on your body is sexy.
MOLLIE: To be kissed on your body?
EMILY: Okay, nobody will kiss me. I'm going to be on a date. I'm going to be on the camping. Tell Derek it's time for me to go to bed when he comes here, all right?
MOLLIE: Does he come to the camping?
EMILY: If he comes here when we sleep he might take me, right?
MOLLIE: This is my pillow. My baby is on the pillow with me.

Second Day

EMILY: This time I'm not having boyfriends.
MOLLIE: Why?
EMILY: Okay, I will.
MARGARET: Am I still the Derek?

EMILY: I'm taking my baby along. A lot of boyfriends are in this room. I'm moving to the other room. Come on, sisters. Let's take all the clothes into the other room. *(The girls move armfuls of clothing and purses to the cubby room.)*

MOLLIE: Does the boyfriend find us?

EMILY: We're packing up and we're going because we don't want boyfriends anymore. There's no girlfriends here. Only there could be sisters.

MARGARET: We don't like boyfriends anymore, right, Emily? So we're moving to sisters?

MOLLIE: We need a mother to pretend. We need a real mother. For the moving. You can't move without a mother to know where you are. Call me the mother only for now.

EMILY: Goodbye, mother. We're not going to come here again. I don't like my boyfriend. Derek wants to do something I don't know what it is.

MARGARET: I'm tired, mother. Cover me up. Put my baby here.

THIRD DAY

EMILY: We're going on a camping and we're going to stay there. I'll call your boyfriends and tell them.

MOLLIE: Who?

EMILY: Derek. Do you still love him?

MOLLIE: Who?

EMILY: Derek. Does he still love you?

MOLLIE: Who?

EMILY: Derek. But don't let him see me because I'm a very little girl now. I used to be big.

MARGARET: Who's the boyfriend that doesn't like you anymore? Mollie could be it.

EMILY: Oh no, he wants to come! Derek wants to come! Oh, no, he's coming!

MOLLIE: *(Frightened)* You better hide.

MARGARET: Call your boyfriend that doesn't love you anymore. Tell him we're on a camping trip!
EMILY: Mollie! Your boyfriend is here! Excuse me. We can't have you for this place because the girls are sleeping here. Oh, no! The boyfriend stoled all our clothes. Oh, no, my purse is stoled!
MOLLIE: Oh no, my dress is gone!
MARGARET: The fire is out. He took the fire out! He took the rug out so the fire will come out. Call the police. There he's coming in here!
EMILY: Help me, help me! He's just a real bad guy! Mollie, did you see that? A bad guy! Hit him with the purse.
MOLLIE: Oh no! Bad guy, bad guy, bad guy, bad guy!

Their screams ricochet through the room. They begin throwing clothing and purses at the unseen villain, then fall into one another's arms, aglow with fright and relief.

"Girls, girls, sh-sh. Too loud. Look, you're tearing that dress." The comforting intrusion of maternal nagging penetrates the barrier. Smiling uncertainly the girls run to my side. Here is the teacher, this is the classroom, the bad guy part is over.

"I think I hear a birthday," Mollie says. "I heard someone laughing over there. I think it's for me."

"Maybe they're laughing because the bad guy is gone," I suggest.

"There wasn't even a bad guy," Margaret says. "We weren't playing that."

Mollie nods. "We went to the camping."

Their anxiety has been too great to allow instant recall. But fantasy play has performed its yeoman service, and the comforted players begin their party preparations. The girls' antidote for fright often comes in the form of royal personages and glittering splendor.

"I'm Princess Sleeping Beauty," Emily says. "Pretend it's my birthday and you have to wake me up with a kiss."

"Am I the prince?" asks Mollie.

"You can be the prince or the queen or the sister,"

answers Emily. "Pretend we're all queens and princes and kings in gold."

"Pretend I'm the queen of silver and jewels," Margaret says. "And you're my children who are Sleeping Beauty princesses. And ruby red."

"And we have glass slippers," Mollie adds. "And there's no chimney."

28

Carrie does not attempt to enter the boyfriend story, but she follows its unfolding closely from the story table. Suddenly her own private anxiety emerges, and she initiates an unexpected drama that is immediately taken up by a number of children in the class. It could be called "Bad Things Happen When Mommy and Daddy Go to Work."

She dictates a series of stories (one a day) in which sisters become naughty as soon as their parents leave for work. In each story a safety rule is flouted and the children are hurt: they play with nails and stick themselves; they climb on the table and fall off; they use a sharp knife and bleed profusely. The format is consistent; only the manner of disobedience and the punishment vary. In some stories the girls are sent to their rooms, and in others the harmful effect of a dangerous act seems punishment enough, as in the following story.

> Once upon a time there was a mother, a father, and four little girls. The father said, "Get up. We're going to work. You stay home by yourself." So they got up and the mother and father went to work. Then they took out their blocks and played with them. They made them so high that they fell on their heads, and there

> wasn't ice to put on the bumps. Then the mother and father came home and saw what they had did. They lived happily ever after.

Mollie is inspired by Carrie's story and transposes it into doll corner play at once.

"Pretend we're sisters," she begins, "and we don't have a father and our mother is at work."

"No, I'm the mother," Carrie says, putting on a blue bonnet.

"Pretend I'm the big girl teenager and you could be the baby that does a bad thing . . ."

"I'm the mother, Mollie."

"Pretend I'm the college girl teenager and . . ."

Carrie is adamant. "I'm the mother and I go to work and I say 'Get up' and you lie down because I have to tell you to get up and I'm going to work."

"But who will be my sister? Pretend I'm the big sister and the brown doll is the baby and the baby tears the telephone paper and calls a false alarm and then . . ." Mollie pauses for a breath.

"Then you call me," Carrie continues, "and you say, 'Come home, mother. The baby did a bad thing.' "

Meanwhile, at the story table, Barney concocts revisions and additions. His sibling characters also do a bad thing when the parents go to work, but their actions quickly become heroic, and the parents, upon returning home, join the adventure.

> First came a daddy. Then came a mommy. Then a brother. Then two little girls. Their mother and father went to work and left them alone. They played with needles. Then a four-headed monster came. Then the mommy and daddy came home. The children defended themselves with the needles and killed the monster dead. Then the mother and father kicked the monster out of the house.

Barney's enlargement of Carrie's text makes me curious about the girls' doll corner version, which Carrie and Mollie have now moved into the blocks. It would appear that I have missed a scene or two.

MOLLIE: Pretend it's starting to rain. It really *is* raining outside. But pretend it's starting to rain in the pretend. Oh-oh! Lots of foxes. I'm going to chase them all away. You stay in the house, mother. Some really bad foxes. They might try to eat you up. Lock up the mushroom house, quick!
CARRIE: They might try to eat *you* up, sister.
MOLLIE: Uh-uh. They can't. I'm a big college girl.
CARRIE: Well, they can't eat a mother. *I'll* scare them away because that's what mothers do. Because foxes like blood. They like to smell it.
MOLLIE: They're all gone. They smelled the mushrooms.
CARRIE: Did you kill the fox?
MOLLIE: Yeah, I did. How about if we creep out of bed and find each other and we can go to the store and get lots of things. And it's night and everyone is asleep. Let's just pretend, okay? Just pretend everyone is asleep.
CARRIE: But first I have to come home from work and . . . should I get angry because there's foxes?
MOLLIE: Yeah, and because the baby broke the telephone so I couldn't call you and then pretend I buyed you a new telephone and you smile when you see it. And then we go hunting.
CARRIE: What are we hunting for?
MOLLIE: For dress-ups. Let's go hunting in the doll corner for dress-ups. Two for you and two for me.
BARNEY: Can I play?
MOLLIE: You could be the father. Pretend we buyed a pumpkin and you're the father and you go to work and me and Carrie are sisters and we don't have a mother and pretend we break the pumpkin and you

say we can't have any presents or else we can't break pumpkins.

CARRIE: First we're asleep and you say, "Get up," and we get up and you go to work.

BARNEY: Don't get into trouble stuff, but then you do.

The peregrinations of a theme continue. Carrie has unleashed a familiar anxiety and given it dramatic expression: something bad will happen if your parents go away. And she has more to say on the subject. What if the father stays home and the mother goes to work?

> Once upon a time there was a mother, a father, and two little girls. The father said, "Get up. Your mother is going to work." And so they got up and the mother went to work. But the father stayed home. But he wasn't in the room where they was at and they played with the can opener and their finger got opened. Then the father saw what they had did and he told the mother. And the mother said, "Go to your room." And they lived happily ever after.

"Carrie, who stays with you when your parents go to work?" I ask.

"The babysitter."

"Did you ever get hurt when your parents were at work?"

"No."

"Did you think you might get hurt?"

"In a dream I did. In a dream it really happened."

"Ah, a dream. The stories are from a dream."

"I really did dream that. And then I telled it to you in a story."

Several days later, Carrie reveals another dream. "Mommy knows it's called a nightmare," she says. "But this one is not to write down because I'm just telling you this one for hearing it."

"Is it too scary to act out?"

Carrie nods. "This is really mommy and daddy and me because this is how I dreamed it. And then the daddy said, 'There are going to be some people who are bringing guns to kill us.' So they had to hide. Then the bad people came. Three people. They had guns. I'm going to do the rest tomorrow. Because I'm too sleepy."

"That's a very scary dream, Carrie. Would you like me to read you a book so you can think about something else?"

"No. I just want to be by myself so I can think about something else."

After a while, Carrie sits beside me at the story table. "Can I do a story?" she asks. "It's about my Cabbage Patch." She has found a whole inventory of something else to think about to erase the memory of three people with guns coming to kill her.

> Once upon a time my Cabbage Patch came. My baby Cabbage Patch was learning how to walk. We went to school together. It was baby school. Then She-Ra came. And then She-Ra and Frosta rided on Swiftwind. And the mother and the Cabbage Patch did too. And they went to He-Man's castle. And there was cookies and tea on the table. And the mother and Cabbage Patch turned into two queens and it was the mother queen's birthday.

There is a sigh of pleasure from others at the table as Carrie finishes her story. Bad guys and monsters depart momentarily while the sweetness of Carrie's fantasy settles over the group.

"You know, Carrie," Fredrick says, "if you're a mother you have two birthdays. You know why? Because you have a birthday when your baby is born."

"Do you mean that the mother has a birthday on the day she was born," I ask, "and also on the day her baby is born?"

"Yeah. Else how could she be a mother?"

"Is that what you think, Carrie?" I ask.

She smiles at Fredrick. "If the mother is a queen she could."

29

The next day, Fredrick dictates a story about a magic person.

> Once there was a magic person who was a wish fairy. The baby wanted a toy so he called up the wish fairy to bring him a toy. So the wish fairy waved his hand three or two times. Whoosh. There was the toy. A cement mixer that was what he wanted.

Christopher does not care much for Fredrick's wish fairy. We hear about it in his next story.

> Once a tiger came. Then the wish fairy. He punched away the wish fairy.

Fredrick is unconcerned. "A real wish fairy can't be punched, you know, Christopher. He could just disappeared."

"Yeah, then the tiger could disappeared where the wish fairy was." Christopher laughs at his own cleverness.

"Ha-ha yourself. Because tigers can't be a magic person. Teacher, what do you say if tigers can be magic or not? Can they?"

"I don't know the answer to that, but I was wondering about something else. Can a wish fairy make a wish for himself?"

"Sure. Here's what I wished in my dream. I wished I was the baby and the baby was the daddy." Fredrick examines my face for a reaction. "Wasn't that a funny thing to wish?"

"People do wish things like that in dreams," I say. "Or

they could pretend it when they play." A few days later, there is a scene of such sweet intimacy between Fredrick and Barney that I wonder if both boys feel they are in a dream.

"Night-night time," Barney says. "Daddy's turning off the light."

"No, let the light on. Baby wants it on."

"But it's already the night."

"Then I have to come in your bed, daddy. No one can see me in my little hideout."

"It's also my hideout because I'm your dad. Careful I don't step on your little toesies. And also watch out for your heady-head, sweet baby. I'm going on the boat now."

"Bye-bye, daddy. Come back and see me sometimes. I can't walk, you know."

"I know. I'll come back since I live with you alone together. Want to sail away with me, darling?"

"No. Bye-bye. See you sometimes."

"Since I live with you, right? I'm living on my boat but sometimes I'll see you again since I like you so much. Pretend this is our pretend Care Bear boat that doesn't rock in the water."

"It's really a cradle, though. Night-night."

The boys have been lying side by side in the large cradle holding hands throughout the dialogue. Barney pushes against the wall to make the cradle rock as Fredrick chants, "Rockabye, rockabye, rockabye."

The reverie is interrupted by Christopher and Stuart, who run through the doll corner shouting, "Ba-ba-boo!"

"Stop being silly," Barney tells them. "This is a Care Bear boat."

"Here, I'm a big wave that comes." Christopher pounces on the cradle and nearly topples it. "How about if I'm the brother bear?"

"No!" Fredrick cries. "Barney is brother bear. I'm the daddy."

"Yeah, I'm the baby," Barney says. "That's all. No more bears are alive in this family."

Barney and Fredrick exchange disguises as if to preserve their secret. Sensing that he is the outsider to an intimate scene, Christopher must do something to alter the balance.

"But there's real danger happening with the police!" he exclaims. "The dragon's getting down in the basement. Quick, father bear, it's a real emergency not pretend. He gots fire!"

Fredrick rouses himself out of the cradle. "Okay, now don't be scared of the dragon. I'm turning into the wish fairy." He blinks twice and shudders effusively. "Magic person, magic person! Wish bad against the dragon! Whoosh! Okay, guys, the dragon is dead. Super-wish fairy fly away!"

30

Having stepped back into the quickened pace of classroom fantasy life, Fredrick happily rediscovers that the choices are abundant and are his alone to make. What he chooses to be, of course, may come in response to someone else's mood. Barney rocks him gently, and he is a loving baby; then Christopher hears a dragon in the basement, and Fredrick must become the all powerful super-wish fairy. This, in turn, leads Christopher to his own superdistraction: the troublesome doll-corner smashie, instigator of the teacher-jailing incident a week earlier.

"Hey, Barn! Doll-corner smashie?" Christopher climbs on the table waving the Raggedy Andy doll and a handful of playdough. "Barney, look at me. This guy's going smashie-poopie all over the room."

As the playdough hits the floor, *my* mood enters the equation. However, remembering my past encounter with doll-corner smashie, I approach carefully.

"What are you playing, boys?"

Christopher senses that my composure is untrustworthy and his excitement increases along with his discomfort. "It's doll-corner smashie!" he squeals.

"Oh, yes. I remember that from last week. There was a bad guy trying to come to your picnic, wasn't there? Is that what's happening now?" I appear to be interested in the drama, but Christopher still doubts my sincerity. He looks at the boys for support. "Mr. Nobody," he blurts out. "I'm Mr. Nobody."

Barney and Fredrick raise their eyebrows appreciatively. Mr. Nobody is Barney's newest storytelling stratagem. "Once Mr. Nobody came" is the way it generally goes, and, when Barney performs the role, no one comes out and nothing happens. The children are delighted and I pretend to be amused. Actually I look upon Mr. Nobody as a new sort of bad guy who has the power to ensnare the entire educational process by doing nothing. Come to think of it, he does a great deal; it is no mean feat to entertain a classroom of children and annoy the teacher all at once.

"Is that the same Mr. Nobody Barney puts in some of his stories?" I ask.

"Yeah, he goes plop, plop, and no one ever sees him, ha, ha."

"Maybe so, Christopher, but the playdough *can* be seen and it's a big mess. Fredrick, you were the wish fairy before. That's a helpful person. Why don't you help Christopher pick it up?"

Fredrick will not be trapped so easily. "I'm Mr. Nobody too," he tells me, and goes over to Christopher's side of the room.

"Well, then, let both Mr. Nobodys pick up the playdough."

Fredrick frowns. "But wait, teacher. If someone is invisible, how can they see the playdough if it's not invisible?"

Fredrick is about to turn a messy floor into a Socratic dialogue. Is he trying to distract me or does his question represent an honest inquiry into the logic of fantasy? Whatever his intention, I shall go along in good faith.

"This is an interesting problem," I say, sitting down at the doll corner table. "Now, let's see. We have two invisible characters who can't see the playdough because *it*'s not invisible."

"Me too,"Barney says eagerly. "I'm Mr. Nobody too."

"All right, *three* invisible characters who can only clean up invisible things. And the playdough is not invisible. So how does it get cleaned up?"

"Yeah, that's the problem!" Christopher's enthusiasm for our newest enigma wipes out all thoughts of doll-corner smashie. The boys have joined me at the table and we look at one another with great seriousness. It is no longer a game of child-teacher-child manipulation; we are using Mr. Nobody's singular attribute—his invisibleness—to solve a real problem of classroom management.

"I know something good," Barney says. "The teacher closes *her* eyes and then if she can't . . . if we can't . . ."

"No, Barn," interrupts Fredrick. "Pretend *everybody* is invisible in this room, even the teacher. Then if everyone is invisible it means the whole doll corner is invisible. See? Then the playdough *has* to be invisible. And we can pick it up."

The idea is accepted instantly. I drop to my knees along with the others and contemplate the novelty of this experience. Yet, is it really new? Fantasy is fulfilling its normal function, creating a world in which the inhabitants solve problems by imagining and describing premises and goals within the context of a dramatic plot.

"What are you doing?" Mollie asks from the doorway.

"You can't come in unless you're invisible," Christopher calls out.

"Why?"

"We're pretending everyone is invisible, Mollie," I explain. "This is how we solved the problem of picking up the playdough if . . ." I falter.

Fredrick comes to my aid. "See, we're Mr. Nobody and he's invisible. And Christopher threw the playdough all over . . ."

"No, not me! Mr. Nobody did it!" Christopher argues. "You have to say Mr. Nobody did it."

He is, of course, correct. The integrity of our task must be maintained, as is always the case with truly satisfying play.

"Never mind," Mollie says. "I have to do something."

"She didn't want to be invisible," I remark, stuffing the last bits of playdough into the container.

"But *we* do, don't we?" Christopher hugs me as hard as he can. He loves it when I behave sensibly.

The whole episode has been geared to making sense. We have modified our various behaviors in order to achieve an intelligent resolution to a problem. The irksome Mr. Nobody, the children's support for Christopher, the messy floor, and my reaction to it are no longer causes for anxiety. Instead they become motivations for telling a story, which is what children know how to do best.

31

I have my own games. "I think Mr. Nobody is a bad guy in disguise," I say at the snack table. The children smile at the idea.

"I know he can't be a good guy," I continue. Now they laugh out loud. Both notions appear ridiculous. Mr. Nobody is outside of categories in an indefinable place.

"Well, what is he then?"

"He's . . . just a . . ."

"Is he a doll-corner smashie?" I ask. The children stare at me in disbelief, then explode into shrieking and chair-toppling. In the moments it takes to settle them down I realize I have touched upon another one of the areas of *not knowing*, where feelings cannot be safely examined.

Yet Mr. Nobody has legitimate precedents: the clown who releases us from the lion tamer's tension, the slapstick comic who bumps into the villain. He also is the school child seeking relief, but unlike the comic and the clown he seldom receives much credit for his performance.

Even the children resist Mr. Nobody if he runs counter to the mood of the group. When the children begin to identify roles and define objectives, Mr. Nobody can be as burdensome to them as to me. Barney and Fredrick have started a robber story that has no room for Mr. Nobody.

"We're robbers, right, Fredrick?"

"I'll be the robber kid, Barney."

"Do robbers have a kid? Okay, I'm the robber head. The guarder. One guarder and one kid."

"Then let me be a robber kid too," Christopher breaks in.

"I mean there can't be robber kids because a kid might have a mother. Mothers can't be robbers."

"Just call me the robber horse," Fredrick decides. "And there's only *one* robber horse."

Christopher feels trapped. "Why can't I be a robber person then? That means just a plain robber. Just the one who does the plain robbing."

"You be the baby robber horse," Barney tells Christopher. "Now listen: Fredrick is your dad and I'm the guard of all the robbers. Now that's *what*."

"Let *me* say what," Christopher argues. "I'll be the . . . mother."

"No! A boy can't be a mother if he's a boy. You have to be the baby horse. We're the boss."

"Ya, ya, I'm a nobody horse. Mr. Nobody's stupid pig. Ya! Ya! I'm a tushie horse. Ya! Ya!"

"You better stop, Christopher," Barney cautions. "If you say Mr. Nobody you can't play."

"Okay, okay. I'll be a robber person who is also the cook. Now that's a good idea, isn't it, Barn?"

"Yeah, we need a cook. I forgot."

As I replay the sequence on the tape recorder it occurs to me that Mr. Nobody's silliness serves a number of useful purposes. Barney and Fredrick sound as if they are deliberately frustrating Christopher, and the sudden intrusion of Mr. Nobody warns them that they are going too far. Crying has a similar effect, but surely Mr. Nobody is a better response. It is a face-saving device and still within the scope of make-believe.

The following day, Mr. Nobody appears again, this time filling an awkward pause when no leader is convincing enough and no bad guy appealing enough to carry the plot forward.

Barney is acting the role of strict father: "Get into bed or I'll spank you, bad children. I have to make breakfast." Barney seems to be off on the wrong track; the disciplinarian is *always* the mother in doll corner play.

"Ba-ba-boo-boo!" Fredrick and Christopher dance around the table making faces.

"Stop that! I'm not kidding."

"Nya-nya-nya."

"Let's wash the dishes, guys," Barney says in a nicer voice.

"Here's your sword, daddy." Fredrick offers him a broom.

"I don't need one. I'm the plain dad."

"Mushy-gushy. You're the mushy-gushy dad. You're the Mr. Nobody yucky dad."

"Mucky-baddy, mucky-daddy."

"I'm not playing with you guys. Good*bye*."

As Barney stomps off, Christopher and Fredrick momentarily increase their giddiness, then grow silent, poking holes in the playdough. What was Mr. Nobody's purpose here? The simple refusal to be bossed without a good story to make it worthwhile?

In any case, there seems nothing lighthearted about Mr. Nobody. His excitement barely covers the sounds of dismay. He is a ship without an anchor, an actor without a script.

32

Barney is particularly skillful at providing anchor and script. It is the mark of his leadership.

"Hey, Fredrick, you wanna see something in my army book that's for me? This, this, and all this armor. And this sword."

Fredrick turns the pages of Barney's book of armaments. "Yeah, but it can't be true, right, Barn?"

"It *is* true. I'm really fighting in the army once. For real. For real!"

"You mean your father?"

"No, no," Barney insists. "He didn't fight in the war. He wasn't married yet with my mom so I fighted alone in the war when I was a Boy Scout alone."

Fredrick struggles with the information. "You mean when you used to be big?"

"Yeah, before I got little again. Hey, you wanna play army, Fredrick?"

The reincarnation theme appears again and again. This time it is not limited to coming alive as oneself or returning as a newborn; Barney adds the possibility of an existence that precedes one's own parents. Clearly the state of nonexistence cannot be imagined.

"Okay, I'll play army if you make me this gun here in the book," Fredrick says. "I'm the army hideout maker and you're the army hideout gun maker."

"I'll try my best," Barney replies. "But don't forget, I didn't used to be a army man for a long time ago."

As the plot develops each actor must be suitably identified, with no loose ends that create a void. Petey, at three, does not yet know everything has to have a name. He sits in a simple three-sided structure moving two small boards up and down.

"What's that you're in, Petey?" Barney asks.

"The same like tomorrow. Because it's the same as the other thing."

"But what's it called?"

"The same as the other thing," Petey repeats.

"What's the name for it?" Barney persists. "Christopher, do you know?"

"I'm not building with him," Christopher answers. "Petey, do you want to connect that to ours?"

"Yeah, mine is that kind of connected," Petey says. "Fredrick, can I have that block over there?"

"Sure. But Petey, what is the *name* that you're inside of?"

"The same thing together."

The boys do not grow impatient. They always assume the other person knows the answer and that it will eventually emerge. The approach is Socratic and no one minds the redundancies or the delay.

"Is it something you drive in it a truck?" Fredrick asks. "A garbage truck?"

"No."

"I know," Christopher says. "Is it a snake space ship?"

"Yeah. A snake space ship. Are you my friend, Christopher?"

"I'm your friend, too, Petey," Barney assures him. "But don't go driving yet. Wait one minute until I finish this gun for Fredrick that he wants it to be for a special army hideout maker man."

Petey whispers to himself, "Special army hideout maker man." It is a magical title full of the promise of exciting events.

"The wheels are moving, captain," Fredrick announces.

"I'm General Neil Armstrong," Barney says.

Christopher uses the new designation immediately. "We're almost in the space runway, General Neil Armstrong."

"Here we go then. We're in the space runway going very fast. Space station over there!"

"Bad guys, bad guys," Petey calls out, looking at Barney for affirmation.

"Not yet, Petey," Barney tells him. "We're doing the part of getting ready. After *that* the bad guys. And after *that* is Neil Armstrong's birthday."

"*Captain General* Neil Armstrong," Petey corrects him.

The "part of getting ready" is, for Barney, greater than the whole. Yet it was he who introduced Mr. Nobody into the classroom. The master plot-maker also is the inventor of a character who defies expectations. To know something is to know its opposites.

Bad guy and birthday are surely opposites. Barney's explanation to Petey clarifies matters for me as well. "No bad guys yet. We're doing the part of getting ready, and after that the bad guys. And after the bad guy is Neil Armstrong's birthday."

The getting ready part is preparation for the bad guy; the more exacting the groundwork the less anxiety while awaiting the crisis. And birthday is the reward. As in a fairy tale, the reward is given to those who overcome danger.

33

I began with the three F's—fantasy, friendship, and fairness—but it is clear to me now that the other side of friendship and fairness is fear, the fear of losing one's special place. Perhaps there never were three F's anyway, since friendship and fairness have little meaning outside of fantasy play.

Petey already knows this. He asks, "Are you my friend?" when Christopher gives him a name for his "same thing together." Who but a friend tells you it is a snake spaceship? And surely any concept of fairness insists that such a ship must be allowed to share General Neil Armstrong's runway.

If there is only one F, it is fantasy, and the Great Book of Fantasy Play has been generous this year in displaying its contents. Even so, there remain many uncut pages. I am certain, for example, that the bad guy represents danger and loss, and that its opposite, birthday, is the affirmation of safety and power; but where do babies fit in?

They are not bad guys, and they do have a good share of the birthdays. Yet babies are surrounded by ambivalence and concern. No matter how many protective devices are maintained, anxiety hovers over the cradle. The demanding, whining creature within seems to embody all the forces that resist separation and socialization. Nostalgic joy constantly mixes with worried anticipation. Unlike bad guy and birthday, baby is an uncertain symbol that changes from class to class and from child to child.

This class has achieved something of a triumph over the enigma with its baby superhero. What combination of factors has put the children in such close touch with the vulnerable side of heroism? Fredrick's overreaction to the birth of a sibling may have been an influence, but, more significantly, there is the continuing need, demonstrated by Barney and Mollie in particular, to accept and integrate conflicting ideas into the ongoing script. As in the theater, the flexibility of the leading actors increases everyone's sensitivity to the nuances of the drama.

Barney was first to speak of baby He-Man, and now, in a new story, we have baby Cringer.

> One day came He-Man. Baby Cringer had a birthday. All his friends came and he opened his presents.

"But when Prince Adam becomes He-Man," I ask, "doesn't Cringer change to Battle Cat?"

"Babies don't have to change. They can always stay a baby. And he has two fathers whoever he wants, Prince Adam or He-Man. Hey, Mollie, you wanna play baby Cringer?"

"Am I mother Cringer?" she asks.

"Yeah, and I'm baby Cringer and it's my birthday."

"Do you need brothers?" Fredrick asks. "Me and Christopher? Hey brother, the bees are eating the cake."

"Don't eat up the cake, bees," Christopher says gruffly. "Pretend there's really bees. Pretend we scared them away."

The boys run about "spraying" bees. "K-shsh, K-shsh!"

"Stop, bees!" cries Fredrick. "This is cake Orko. I'm King Orko. You're the Orko people."

"Except me. I'm baby Cringer."

"Wait, baby Cringer! Mother, cover the baby. They're going to destroy the world. But I got the magic bomb. Poooshsh! Gone into the universe!"

"Here's your new cake, baby Cringer," Mollie says. "Give him the presents."

"Can I open them?"

"You don't have to *ask* at your birthday," Christopher says. "All the everything is for you."

"Wow! Thanks a lot."

"Orko!" Christopher shouts. "I think we better go hunting turkeys. You too, baby Cringer. You already learned how to crawl. First prize goes to baby Cringer. A golden egg."

Barney does not want to age so quickly. "How about if I'm still sleeping and you're holding your ray gun and you don't want to wake me up and there's a bad guy somewhere and you don't want me to be afraid because I'm so tiny and I didn't start to crawl yet."

"This is a job for King Orko! I'll use my transformer, Barney. Or I could use a sword. Christopher, you guard the house."

"It's almost time for my birthday, everyone. If anybody comes, see who it is." Barney ducks under the blanket.

"Don't worry about a thing, little baby. You want to go to Florida for your birthday? We don't have enough money but this ticket will give us enough money. As soon as we get the money we'll go to Florida a few days later."

"Thanks, dad. You're my dad, Fredrick. King Orko is my dad."

"Open your presents, baby Battle Cat."

"Now am I baby Battle Cat, Fredrick?"

"Because I can do magic." Fredrick waves a cardboard wand. "I changed my name from Orko to He-Man. And you're my baby. So it's really happy birthday to baby Battle Cat. Did I give you a good surprise?"

Barney jumps up and hugs Fredrick. "What a surprise! This is my favorite surprise in my whole life!"

"Then can I be baby Cringer now, Barn?" Fredrick asks. "It's my turn."

"Okay. And you can decide who you want for a dad. Do you want Prince Adam or He-Man?"

Fredrick sits on the floor and wrinkles his brow. "I want . . . two dads . . . and also two mothers . . . and also I want a hundred and twenty-two surprises. And make it only *my* birthday, nobody else can have one."

"You mean on *this* day. Because everyone has to have a birthday," Barney says. "If God wants them to. Because God always wants people to have presents all for theirselfs."

"But not bad guys," Fredrick says.

Christopher speaks up. "Wait a minute, Fredrick. Let's have it this way. Let's say, pretend you're a bad guy and then you could have a *pretend* birthday."

"Okay," Fredrick agrees solemly. "Only if God wants it."

34

Petey has been watching the older boys vie for the role of baby Cringer. His own mood is quite different.

"Feel this how strong," Petey says, flexing his arm an inch from my face. "That's because it's my birthday."

"Happy birthday, Petey. M-m-m. It does feel strong."

"Do my story first because it's my birthday."

> Once there was Mighty Mouse. And he had his birthday from now. And he got very strong on his birthday. And he ate a lot of spinach on his birthday. And a lot of cake. A person that is a wolf came. And Mighty Mouse said, "I'm stronger than you, wolf." Then Mighty Mouse throwed him out of the window. Then Mighty Mouse flied out of the window and he's really Super Mighty Mouse.

"How old are you, Petey?" Fredrick asks.

"Four. That's a big boy."

"But I'm bigger, right, Petey? Because don't you remember when it was my birthday I was already bigger?"

Petey stands alongside Fredrick and look up at him with a steady gaze. "You wanna be the wolf in my story, Fredrick?"

"Okay. What's he do?"

"He hasta gets throwed out of the window. Super Mighty Mouse throwed him out."

"Can I be Super Mighty Mouse?" Fredrick asks.

"No, I have to because when it's your birthday because you're stronger on your birthday."

Fredrick must know this rule about birthdays but Petey can invent it for himself now. He calls over to Barney in the blocks. "Don't fly yet. Wait for the teacher has to make me a cape. Teacher, hurry up. Can you make me a cape it says 'Super Mighty Mouse R' "?

I print his message on a long piece of paper and ask, "What does the R mean?"

"It means flying. You only have it on a birthday."

Petey may have just presented a preview of next year's theater bill. He'll be in the "olderest" group then, inventing new rules and symbols and doubtless reorganizing the bad guys, birthdays, and babies into another configuration of Great Ideas.

There are further intimations of the coming year. Jonathan, who walks the line between three and four, dictates a story in which he is the female hero (not uncommon for a younger boy) but then launches into a rather mature dialogue on the subject of bad guys.

> I'm going to be She-Ra. And she can fly. With Swiftwind. Then she goes "Huff-huff" because she falls on her feet. She has a cape too. She can disappear.

"I didn't know that She-Ra can disappear," I comment.

"Oh, yeah, she really could," Jonathan replies. "And Skeletor doesn't and Hordak doesn't. Not the bad guys don't."

"Only the good guys disappear? I wonder why."

Jonathan is certain of the answer. "Because the good guys don't want to see the bad guys!"

"And do the bad guys want to see the good guys?" I ask.

"Yes, yes! So they will get them."

Fredrick interprets for Jonathan. "He means the good guys will get the bad guys, right, Jonathan?"

"That's what I said. Because they can disappear."

"He means the *good* guys can disappear," Fredrick explains. I think back to Fredrick's own attempt months earlier to describe the good guy–bad guy dilemma, and the measure of his growth seems enormous.

"I see. So, if the bad guys can't disappear then the good guys will know where they are. Is that what you mean, Jonathan?" I ask.

"And the good guys don't want to see the bad guys," he repeats.

"Wait, *I'll* say what he means!" Fredrick is clearly enjoying his role as senior adviser. "He means the good guys can disappear if they don't want to see the bad guys, but if they *do* want to, in case they're hiding, then they don't have to disappear if they don't want to. Isn't that right, Jonathan?"

Jonathan smiles at Fredrick and hugs his arm. "Are you my friend, Fredrick?"

"Yeah, I am. Hey, me and Barney are going to look for strangers in the cubby room. You wanna be on our team?"

"No," he answers, his smile changing to a frown. "I don't want to have strangers in the cubby room."

"I mean we're pretending."

"I don't want you to pretend that."

"It's okay, Jonathan," I say. "You don't need to pretend that. They can pretend by themselves."

Jonathan's bad guy logistics are not intended to be acted out in cubby rooms. They are for thinking and dreaming and storytelling, but he does not wish to find out what might happen when you go looking for them in the cubby room.

Fredrick and Barney, of course, have discovered that since it is they who put the strangers in the cubby room, *they* can decide the degree of danger involved. Even so, after a brief interlude, the explosive sounds in the cubby room suggest a spiraling loss of control, and I am not surprised to see Christopher running toward me in dismay.

"Hurry up! Come in there!" he shouts, pulling my arm with both hands. "Look what they're doing!"

The cubby room is a disaster; coats and jackets are strewn everywhere as the boys continue to pull them down and stomp on them. "They're under here! We trapped the strangers! Smoosh 'em! Smoosh 'em!"

"Stop, boys, stop right now! You can't pretend this way. Will you please hang up the clothes. This is too big a mess."

"The strangers were hiding behind there," Barney huffs.

"You were *pretending* they were behind there. But, look at what you're doing. You're stepping on people's coats."

"Yeah, but people won't mind because they don't like strangers to be behind their stuff."

"You mean pretend strangers."

"Yeah. They neither want pretend strangers behind their stuff."

The territory is familiar, in between their world and mine. "Are the pretend strangers gone?" I ask.

"We locked them in jail."

"Good. Then I'll read the names and you find the coats and hang them up. It might be a hard job for you."

"Not too hard for us," Fredrick says. "Superdetectives could tell people's things with X-ray eyes."

35

Fredrick has a problem the next day, however, that cannot immediately be solved by a superdetective. He stands in the doorway clinging to his mother, who has a diaper bag in one hand, a purse in the other, and a baby carrier strapped to her chest. "Fredrick wants me to stay for a bit," she says without conviction.

Several children rush to see the sleeping infant, partially hidden by the flap of his canvas pouch. "Why do you hang the baby on your front?" Mollie asks. "My mommy putted Leslie in a backpack."

"Maybe we'll do that when Stevie is older. Where shall I sit, Fredrick?"

He leads his mother to a big chair in the corner and squeezes into a doubtful space on her lap. She moves the carrier to give Fredrick more room but quickly urges, "Aren't you going to play? You said you wanted me to watch you play, honey."

"I got too tired now, mommy. I want to rest by the baby."

"Can I see your brother?" Barney asks. "I can't tell how his face looks."

"He's not my brother. He's the baby. And he doesn't want people to know what his face looks!"

Barney glances questioningly at Fredrick's mother. "Stevie is sleeping now, Barney. If he wakes up you'll see him then. Why don't you boys build something nice and I'll watch you."

"Hey, yeah, Fredrick. Let's make a ship, okay?"

"I'm too tired for that."

"Tell you what, honey. I'll read you and Barney a book and after that you can build a ship. How about that?"

"Not Barney. Just me." He scrambles off her lap and returns in a moment with three books.

"Well, honey, if this is what you want, okay. But, Fredrick, listen. When I finish these I'll have to leave. Promise me you'll be good."

He nods imperceptibly and nuzzles into the baby's blanket, sucking on a corner ribbon and his own thumb at the same time. His mother reads softly, knowing he wants her words to be for him alone. As she nears the end of the last book, Fredrick throws his arms around her neck and pleads, "Don't go, mommy. Stay with me another minute!"

"Oh, honey, you promised you wouldn't make a fuss. I'm really disappointed."

At this, he dissolves into tears. "Take me home, mommy! Please! I wanna go with you. Please, mommy! I'm too tired today."

A hush descends on the room; everyone stops to watch Fredrick and his mother. The children recognize Fredrick's panic and seem to hold their breaths.

"Why not let him go with you," I suggest. "He does look rather worn out, don't you think?"

Fredrick grins tearfully and races to the cubby room.

"We'll play with you tomorrow, okay, Fredrick?" I say, zipping his jacket. The children surround him with sympathetic murmurs, then return to their play in a renewed spirit. A real emergency has occurred and they must hurry to disguise their stirred up feelings.

A smiling Fredrick arrives early the next morning bearing a Superman doll. "Look what I brang, teacher! I gots two but this one is my favorite one I like better because he can fly better like this. Watch me how he goes."

Fredrick circles the table, holding his little red and blue figure aloft; there seems to be no residue of yesterday's unhappy scene.

"Can I be first on the story list? I'm the real Superman and this is baby Superman." During the entire storytelling that follows, Fredrick's eyes are fixed on his doll. He moves its arms and legs continually, altering their position from sitting to walking to flying. There is the sense of an inner dialogue between doll and boy even as the words of a story pour forth.

> First Superman came. Then he flied around. Then he spotted a little baby Superman. "You want to fly with me, baby Superman?" Then a witch came and throwed a net on Superman and baby Superman. Then Spiderman came and he sprayed a net on the witch.

"Am I in your story?" Mollie asks.

"Who do you want to be? The witch?"

"No. I'll be Superwoman."

"Oh. She didn't come in my story yet. I'll tell the teacher. Do you want Superwoman to kill the witch, Mollie?"

Mollie considers the possibilities. "Can I be the one who holds baby Superman?"

"Sure. Hey, guess what, Mollie! Pretend I'm the Superman dad and you're the Superwoman mom and we make the baby a little house, okay?"

"And a tiny tiny tiny bed," Mollie hums.

"For his tiny tiny tiny head," Fredrick sings along. The printed story is forgotten as the real drama begins.

Fredrick kneels beside Mollie, watching her tuck the Superman doll into an empty chalk box. He reaches out to stroke her hair, moving his lips in a silent message. Then, as if summoned by a distant alarm, he springs up and whirls around. "Did you hear a noise in the chimney, mother?"

"In the woods. I heared one in the woods."

"Good. I'll put on my cape and see if some trouble is coming." He stops to draw an S on a sheet of paper. "Tape this quick, teacher!"

"Hey, c'mere, Fredrick," Barney summons from the sand table. "Slimy potion! Y'wanna help us? It could make everyone die. The whole city. Right, Christopher?"

"Yeah, it's kryptonite. Superman can die in this."

Fredrick squirms away, his cape only partially fastened. "You're wrong, Christopher. Superman doesn't die from kryptonite. He doesn't *ever* die."

"Everyone dies forever, you know," Barney reminds him.

Suddenly, Fredrick's concern is power, power over life and death. He turns from Mollie's domestic scene and strides to the sand table. "Superman the real Superman can make the spell work forever," he declares in a deepened voice.

Barney pours in more water. "This is the spell," he whispers. The boys laugh at the widening pool forming in the sand and ooze their fingers through it, murmuring "slimy potion, slimy potion."

"I gotta idea," Fredrick says. "When I put a power on your arm it turns to a power to a bat and it goes to fight people and it carries them back to the castle. O-kay-Barney-bat-o-kay-Christopher-bat-you-will-carry-people-back-to-the-castle-you-will-destroy-the-people."

Instantly undertaking their new roles, the boys flap their

sandy arms and fly around the table. “Argh! Argh! Argh! Master, master, it’s working. The formula’s working!”

Fredrick nods approvingly. “Good. You’re the helpfullest bats there ever was. Go-get-me-three-a-hundred-sharks!”

“Here, master. What you want. They’re wet to a death.”

“But if I touch anyone they could come back to life,” Fredrick sings. “Back to life, wet to a death, back to life!”

“Help, help!” Barney screams. “I’m destroying! The king! The invisible bad king! He told me to get you. If I don’t he’ll put glue all over me. I’m turning to a statue! Now I’m all chained up. I’m in glue prison!”

“Don’t worry, Barney bat. I’ll save you. Here, I’m melting you with my face. There! Now break yourself out.”

“Whew! Thanks, Fredrick. You saved me. I was starting to die. Now I can live for the whole forever.”